Bibliography of Published Works
by Kenneth E. Boulding

Bibliography of Published Works by Kenneth E. Boulding

Compiled by Vivian L. Wilson

with the assistance of Susan Dunahay

Introduction by Kenneth E. Boulding

COLORADO ASSOCIATED UNIVERSITY PRESS

Published by Colorado Associated University Press
Boulder, Colorado 80309
ISBN 0-87081-140-1
Library of Congress Catalog Card Number 82-074149
Printed in the United States of America

INTRODUCTION

One of the penalties of a long life of writing is that it is often quite difficult to find what one has published . . . and if the author has this difficulty, how much more difficult must it be for the reader. This bibliographic volume provides some solutions to that difficulty, and I am indeed grateful to the Colorado Associated University Press for publishing it. Even those who disagree with me may find this volume an excellent guide to my literary or scientific misdemeanors, and I hope they will take advantage of it and criticize me accordingly, as I have found no faster process of learning.

The patience and skill which have been put into this volume by its compiler, my secretary and administrative assistant, Mrs. Vivian Wilson, are beyond measurement. In a sense she increased her own task, for had it not been for the constant help and encouragement which she has given me these last eighteen years, the bibliography would have been much shorter. I am grateful also for the help given by Mrs. Wilson's assistant, Ms. Susan Dunahay, both for her bibliographic work and meticulous typing. If anything is ever discovered which is missing from this volume, I shall be much surprised, but we are always on the lookout for elusive publications!

I am a compulsive writer (I once almost thought of forming a Writers' Anonymous for people like myself) and at the age of seventy-five I seem to be aging quite slowly, so I cannot guarantee that this volume is final. Indeed, I shall look forward to a new edition in 1995. And in the meantime, again, my thanks to the people who have made this volume possible.

Kenneth E. Boulding
Distinguished Professor of Economics Emeritus
Institute of Behavioral Science
University of Colorado, Boulder
July 1985

CONTENTS

BIBLIOGRAPHY OF PUBLISHED WORKS

Key: CP -- Reprinted in **Kenneth E. Boulding Collected Papers I-VI**
BE -- Reprinted in **Beyond Economics**
RI -- Further reprint information available from the author

1932

ARTICLES

The Place of the "Displacement Cost" Concept in Economic Theory. **Economic Journal**, 42, 165 (Mar. 1932): 137-141. CP I, pp. 1-7.

The Possibilities of Socialism in Britain. **Plan** (Exeter College, Oxford), 1, 4 (May 1932): 25-27.

1934

ARTICLE

The Application of the Pure Theory of Population Change to the Theory of Capital. **Quarterly Journal of Economics**, 48 (Aug. 1934): 645-666. CP I, pp. 9-32.

1935

ARTICLES

A Note on the Consumption Function. **Review of Economic Studies**, 2, 2 (Feb. 1935): 99-103. CP I, pp. 33-39.

The Theory of a Single Investment. **Quarterly Journal of Economics**, 49, 3 (May 1935): 475-494. CP I, pp. 41-62.

1936

ARTICLES

Professor Knight's Capital Theory: A Note in Reply. **Quarterly Journal of Economics,** 50, 3 (May 1936): 524-531.

Time and Investment. **Economica,** NS 3, 10 (May 1936): 196-220. CP I, pp. 63-89. Reply. **Economica,** NS 3, 12 (Nov. 1936): 440-442.

1937

BOOK REVIEW

Review of E.C. van Dorp, A Simple Theory of Capital, Wages, and Profit or Loss. **Economic Journal** 47, 187 (Sept. 1937): 522-524.

1938

ARTICLES AND PAMPHLET

An Experiment in Friendship. **American Friend,** 26, 26 (Dec. 22, 1938): 541-542.

In Defense of the Supernatural. **Friends Intelligencer,** 95, 41 (Oct. 8, 1938): 677-678.

Making Education Religious. **American Friend,** 26, 20 (Sept. 29, 1938): 408-409.

Paths of Glory: A New Way With War (pamphlet). Glasgow: University Press, for the John Horniman Trust, 1938. 32 pp.

Worship and Fellowship. **Friends Intelligencer,** 95, 35 (Aug. 27, 1938): 579-580.

BOOK REVIEW

Review of W.L. Valk, Production, Pricing, and Unemployment in the Static State. **Economic Journal,** 48, 189 (Mar. 1938): 92-93.

1939

ARTICLES

Equilibrium and Wealth: A Word of Encouragement to Economists. **Canadian Journal of Economics and Political Science,** 5, 1 (Feb. 1939): 1-18. CP I, pp. 91-110.

In Praise of Maladjustment. **Friends Intelligencer,** 96, 32 (Aug. 12, 1939): 519-520. RI.

A Pacifist View of History. **Fellowship,** 5, 3 (Mar. 1939): 10-11.

BOOK REVIEW

Quantitative Economics. Review of John R. Hicks, Value and Capital, An Inquiry into Some Fundamental Principles of Economic Theory; and Henry Schultz, The Theory of Measurement of Demand. **Canadian Journal of Economics and Political Science,** 5, 4 (Nov. 1939): 521-528.

1940

ARTICLES

In Praise of Selfishness. **Friends Intelligencer,** 97, 9 (Mar. 2, 1940): 131-132.

The Pacifism of All Sensible Men. **Friends Intelligencer,** 97, 50 (Dec. 14, 1940): 801.

A Service of National Importance. **American Friend,** 28, 25 (Dec. 5, 1940): 521-522.

Some Reflections on Stewardship. **American Friend,** NS 28, 22 (Oct. 24, 1940): 452-454.

What Lies Ahead? **The Colgate Maroon,** 72, 177 (May 20, 1940): 1.

1941

ARTICLE

The Economics of Reconstruction. **American Friend,** 29, 9 (Apr. 24, 1941): 177-178.

BOOK

Economic Analysis. New York: Harper & Brothers, 1941. xviii + 809 pp. See also: Books, 1948, 1955, 1966.

1942

ARTICLES AND PAMPHLETS

The Abolition of Membership. **American Friend**, 30, 17 (Aug. 13, 1942): 350-351.

A Deepening Loyalty. **Friend** (London), 115, 26 (June 25, 1942): 467-468.

In Praise of Danger. **Friend** (London), 100, 2 (Jan. 9, 1942): 9-10.

New Nations for Old (Pendle Hill Pamphlet No. 17). Wallingford, Pa.: Pendle Hill, 1942. 40 pp.

The Practice of the Love of God (William Penn Lecture; pamphlet). Philadelphia: Religious Society of Friends, 1942. 31 pp.

Taxation in War Time: Some Implications for Friends. **American Friend**, 30, 8 (Apr. 9, 1942): 152-167.

The Theory of the Firm in the Last Ten Years. **American Economic Review**, 32, 4 (Dec. 1942): 791-802. CP I, pp. 111-124.

What Is Loyalty? (reflections on "A Statement of Loyalty Issued by Members of the Society of Friends," Mar. 28, 1918). **Friends Intelligencer**, 99, 27 (July 4, 1942): 425-426.

1943

ARTICLE

The Problem of the Country Meeting. **Friends Intelligencer**, 100, 46 (Nov. 13, 1943): 748-749.

1944

ARTICLES

Desirable Changes in the National Economy After the War (presentation at the American Farm Economic Association meeting, St. Louis, Sept. 1943). **Journal of Farm Economics**, 26, 1 (Feb. 1944): 95-100. CP I, pp. 125-132.

The Incidence of a Profits Tax. **American Economic Review**, 34, 3 (Sept. 1944): 567-572. CP I, pp. 145-152.

Is It the System or Is It You? **Highroad** (Nov. 1944): 14-17.

A Liquidity Preference Theory of Market Prices. **Economica**, NS 11, 42 (May 1944): 55-63. CP I, pp. 133-143. RI.

Nationalism, Millennialism and the Quaker Witness. **American Friend**, 32, 20 (Oct. 5, 1944): 397-398.

Personal and Political Peacemaking: Application of the Friends Peace Testimony. **American Friend**, 32, 17 (Aug. 24, 1944): 347-348.

BOOK REVIEW

Review of Robert A. Brady, Business as a System of Power. **Journal of Land & Public Utility Economics** (Feb. 1944): 85.

VERSE

The Nayler Sonnets. **Inward Light,** 19 (Spring 1944): 4-13. Also published as: There Is a Spirit (The Nayler Sonnets). New York: Fellowship Press, 1945. 26 pp.

1945

ARTICLES

The Concept of Economic Surplus. **American Economic Review**, 35, 5 (Dec. 1945): 851-869. Errata. **American Economic Review**, 36, 3 (June 1946): 393. CP I, pp. 191-211. RI.

The Consumption Concept in Economic Theory. **American Economic Review** (Papers and Proceedings of the 57th American Economic Association annual meeting, Washington, D.C., Feb. 1945), 35, 2 (May 1945): 1-14. CP I, pp. 153-168.

The Home as a House of Worship. **Inward Light,** 27 (Nov. 1945): 6-8.

In Defense of Monopoly. **Quarterly Journal of Economics,** 59, 4 (Aug. 1945): 524-542. CP I, pp. 169-189. Reply. **Quarterly Journal of Economics,** 60, 4 (Aug. 1946): 619-621.

The Prayer of Magic and the Prayer of Love. **Friends Intelligencer,** 102, 15 (Apr. 14, 1945): 235-236.

Times and Seasons. **Friends Intelligencer,** 102, 6 (Feb. 10, 1945): 88.

Where Is the Labor Movement Moving? **Kiwanis Magazine,** 30, 2 (Feb. 1945): 11, 31-32.

BOOKS

The Economics of Peace. New York: Prentice-Hall, 1945. ix + 277 pp. Translations: French, German, Japanese, Spanish. Reissued: Freeport, New York: Books for Libraries Press, 1972. 260 pp.

There Is a Spirit (The Nayler Sonnets). See also: Verse, 1944.

1946

ARTICLE

In Defense of Monopoly: Reply. See: Articles, 1945.

BOOK REVIEWS

The Nature of Communist Crisis. Review of Alexander Baykov, The Development of the Soviet Economic System. **Nation,** 163 (July 27, 1946): 102-103.

Reply to Hayek. Review of Herman Finer, Road to Reaction. **Nation,** 162 (Jan. 5, 1946): 22-23.

Standard American Protestantism. Review of Norman E. Nygaard, America Prays. **American Friend,** 34, 23 (Nov. 14, 1946): 455.

1947

ARTICLES

Economic Analysis and Agricultural Policy (presentation at the Canadian Political Science Association meeting, Quebec, May 1947). **Canadian Journal of Economics and Political Science,** 13, 3 (Aug. 1947): 436-446. CP I, pp. 219-231.

The Inward Light. **Canadian Friend,** 44, 2 (July 1947): 5-6.

A Note on the Theory of the Black Market. **Canadian Journal of Economics and Political Science,** 13, 1 (Feb. 1947): 115-118. CP I, pp. 213-218. RI.

BOOK REVIEW

Review of Melvin G. DeChazeau, Albert G. Hart, Gardiner Means, Howard B. Myers, Herbert Stein, and Theodore O. Yntema, Jobs and Markets: How to Prevent Inflation and Depression in the Transition (Committee for Economic Development Research Study). **Review of Economic Statistics,** 29, 1 (Feb. 1947): 52-54.

1948

ARTICLES

Comment on Mr. Burk's Note (The Net National Product Concept). **American Economic Review,** 38, 5 (Dec. 1948): 899.

Does Large Scale Enterprise Lower Costs? Discussion (with others). **American Economic Review** (Papers and Proceedings of the 60th American Economic Association annual meeting, Chicago, Dec. 1947), 38, 2 (May 1948): 165-171.

Price Control in a Subsequent Deflation. **Review of Economics and Statistics,** 30, 1 (Feb. 1948): 15-17.

World Economic Contacts and National Policies. In: **The World Community,** Quincy Wright, ed. (papers prepared for the 23rd Harris Foundation Institute, Highland Park, Ill., Mar. 1947). Chicago: University of Chicago Press, 1948, pp. 95-100; discussion, pp. 101-144.

BOOK

Economic Analysis. Revised edition. New York: Harper & Brothers, 1948. xxvi + 884 pp. See also: Books, 1941, 1955, 1966.

BOOK REVIEWS

Samuelson's Foundations: The Role of Mathematics in Economics. Review article of Paul Samuelson, Foundations of Economic Analysis. **Journal of Political Economy,** 56, 3 (June 1948): 187-199. CP I, pp. 233-247.

Professor Tarshis and the State of Economics. Review article of Lorie Tarshis, The Elements of Economics. **American Economic Review,** 38, 1 (Mar. 1948): 92-102.

Review of D. McCord Wright, The Economics of Disturbance. **Review of Economics and Statistics,** 30, 1 (Feb. 1948): 74.

1949

ARTICLES

Collective Bargaining and Fiscal Policy. **Industrial Relations Research Association Proceedings,** 2 (Dec. 1949): 52-68. CP I, pp. 275-291. RI.

The Economic Consequences of Some Recent Antitrust Decisions: Discussion (with others). **American Economic Review** (Papers and Proceedings of the 61st American Economic Association annual meeting, Cleveland, Dec. 1948), 39, 3 (May 1949): 320-321.

Is Economics Necessary? (presentation in the Sciences of Society Symposium at the Centennial Celebration of the American Association for the Advancement of Science, Washington, D.C., Sept. 1948). **Scientific Monthly,** 68, 4 (Apr. 1949): 235-240. BE, pp. 1-13. CP I, pp. 249-261. RI.

The Theory and Measurement of Price Expectations: Discussion (with others). **American Economic Review** (Papers and Proceedings of the 61st American Economic Association annual meeting, Cleveland, Dec. 1948), 39, 3 (May 1949): 167-168.

BOOK REVIEW

Review of Sumner H. Slichter, The American Economy: Its Problems and Prospects. **Annals of the American Academy of Political and Social Science,** 261 (Jan. 1949): 201-202.

1950

ARTICLES AND PAMPHLET

The Background and Structure of a Macro-Economic Theory of Distribution. In: **Economic Theory in Review,** C. Lawrence Christenson, ed. (Social Science Series No. 8). Bloomington: Indiana University Publications, 1950, pp. 68-81.

Income or Welfare? **Review of Economic Studies,** 17 (2), 43 (1949-50): 77-86. CP I, pp. 263-274.

The Models for a Macro-Economic Theory of Distribution. In: **Economic Theory in Review,** C. Lawrence Christenson, ed. (Social Science Series No. 8). Bloomington: Indiana University Publications, 1950, pp. 82-95.

Protestantism's Lost Economic Gospel. **Christian Century,** 67, 33 (Aug. 16, 1950): 970-972.

Religious Perspectives of College Teaching in Economics (pamphlet). New Haven, Conn.: Edward W. Hazen Foundation, 1950. 24 pp. BE, pp. 177-197. RI.

BOOK

A Reconstruction of Economics. New York: John Wiley & Sons, 1950. xii + 311 pp. Translations: Portuguese, Spanish. Paperback edition: New York: Science Editions, 1962.

BOOK REVIEW

Humane Economics. Review of Wilhelm Röpke, The Social Crisis of Our Time. **Christian Century,** 67, 44 (Nov. 1, 1950): 1295.

1951

ARTICLES

Asset Identities in Economic Models. In: **Studies in Income and Wealth,** Vol. 14 (papers from the Conference on Income and Wealth, Apr. 1950). New York: National Bureau of Economic Research, 1951, pp. 229-247; comments, pp. 247-256; reply, pp. 256-258. CP I, pp. 293-311.

Can We Control Inflation in a Garrison State? **Social Action,** 17, 3 (Mar. 15, 1951): 3-24. CP III, pp. 1-24.

Comments (on Professor Dr. Wolfgang F. Stolper, "The Economics of Peace"). **Weltwirtschaftliches Archiv** (Keil, Germany), 66, 1 (1951): 146-147.

Defense and Opulence: The Ethics of International Economics. **American Economic Review** (Papers and Proceedings of the 63rd American Economic Association annual meeting, Chicago, Dec. 1950), 41, 2 (May 1951): 210-220. CP I, pp. 313-325.

Wages as a Share in the National Income. In: **The Impact of the Union: Eight Economic Theorists Evaluate the Labor Union Movement,** D. McCord Wright, ed. (edited report of the Institute on the Structure of the Labor Market, American University, May 1950). New York: Harcourt Brace, 1951, pp. 123-148; discussion, pp. 149-167. CP I, pp. 327-354.

What About Christian Economics? **American Friend,** 39, 23 (Nov. 8, 1951): 361.

BOOK REVIEWS

M. Allais' Theory of Interest. Review article of Maurice Allais, Économie et Intérêt. **Journal of Political Economy,** 59, 1 (Feb. 1951): 69-73.

Review of R.H. Coase, British Broadcasting. **Journal of Higher Education,** 22 (Feb. 1951): 110.

Democracy and the Economic Challenge. Review of the 1950-51 William W. Cook Lectures on American Institutions. **Michigan Alumnus Quarterly Review,** 57, 18 (May 26, 1951): 185-191.

Review of I.M.D. Little, A Critique of Welfare Economics. **Economica** 18, 70 (May 1951): 207-209.

Review of George Kingsley Zipf, Human Behavior and the Principle of Least Effort. **American Economic Review,** 41, 3 (June 1951): 449-450.

1952

ARTICLES

A Conceptual Framework for Social Science. **Papers of the Michigan Academy of Science, Arts, and Letters,** 37 (1952): 275-282. BE, pp. 55-63. CP IV, pp. 1-10.

Economics as a Social Science. In: **The Social Sciences at Mid-Century: Essays in Honor of Guy Stanton Ford.** Minneapolis: University of Minnesota Press, for the Social Science Research Center of the Graduate School, 1952, pp. 70-83. CP III, pp. 25-40.

The Great Revolution (summary of Baltimore Yearly Meeting lecture, Mar. 1952). **Friends Intelligencer,** 109, 17 (Apr. 26, 1952): 231-232.

Implications for General Economics of More Realistic Theories of the Firm. **American Economic Review** (Papers and Proceedings of the 64th American Economic Association annual meeting, Boston, Dec. 1951), 42, 2 (May 1952): 35-44. CP I, pp. 355-366.

Religious Foundations of Economic Progress, **Harvard Business Review,** 30, 3 (May-June 1952): 33-44. BE, pp. 196-211. CP III, pp. 41-51. RI.

Welfare Economics. In: **A Survey of Contemporary Economics,** Vol. II, B. Haley, ed. Homewood, Ill.: Richard D. Irwin, for the American Economic Association, 1952, pp. 1-34; comment, pp. 34-38. CP I, pp. 367-402.

BOOK

Readings in Price Theory, Vol. VI (edited with George J. Stigler). Homewood, Ill.: Richard D. Irwin, for the American Economic Association, 1952. x + 568 pp.

BOOK REVIEWS AND DISCUSSION

Discussion of papers by Daniel H. Brill, "Social Accounting and Economic Analysis"; Ruth P. Mack, "Contrasts in Patterns of Flows of Commodities and Funds"; and Karl Brunner and Harry Markowitz, "Stocks and Flows in Monetary Analysis." **Econometrica,** 20, 3 (July 1952): 497-498.

Memorial Anthology. Review of Arthur F. Burns, ed., Wesley Clair Mitchell, The Economic Scientist. **Scientific Monthly,** 75, 2 (1952): 129-130.

Review of National Bureau of Economic Research, Studies in Income and Wealth, Vol. 13 (Conference on Income and Wealth). **Econometrica,** 20, 1 (Jan. 1952): 107-108.

Shirtsleeve Economics. Review of William A. Paton, Shirtsleeve Economics. **Michigan Alumnus Quarterly Review** (Summer 1952): 360.

Review of Norbert Wiener, The Human Use of Human Beings: Cybernetics and Society. **Econometrica,** 20, 4 (Oct. 1952): 702.

VERSE

The Busted Thermostat. **Michigan Business Review**, 4, 6 (Nov. 1952): 25-26.

1953

ARTICLES

The Contribution of Economics to the Understanding of the Firm--I Marginal Analysis. In: **Contemporary Economic Problems** (Lectures from the Economics-in-Action Program). Cleveland, Ohio: Case Institute of Technology, 1953, pp. 15-27.

The Contribution of Economics to the Understanding of the Firm--II The Theory of Organization and Communications. In: **Contemporary Economic Problems** (Lectures from the Economics-in-Action Program). Cleveland, Ohio: Case Institute of Technology, 1953, pp. 28-40.

Economic Issues in International Conflict (lecture at Vanderbilt University, Dec. 1951). **Kyklos**, 6, 2 (1953): 97-115. CP V, pp. 1-22.

Economic Progress as a Goal in Economic Life. In: **Goals of Economic Life**, Dudley Ward, ed. New York: Harper & Brothers, 1953, pp. 52-83. CP III, pp. 53-86.

The Fruits of Progress and the Dynamics of Distribution. **American Economic Review** (Papers and Proceedings of the 65th American Economic Association annual meeting, Chicago, Dec. 1952), 43, 2 (May 1953): 473-483. CP I, pp. 403-415.

The Quaker Approach in Economic Life. In: **The Quaker Approach**, John Kavanaugh, ed. New York: G.P. Putnam's Sons, 1953, pp. 43-58.

The Skills of the Economist. In: **Contemporary Economic Problems** (Lectures from the Economics-in-Action Program). Cleveland, Ohio: Case Institute of Technology, 1953, pp. 3-14.

Toward a General Theory of Growth (paper presented at the Canadian Political Science Association meeting, London, June 1953). **Canadian Journal of Economics and Political Science**, 19, 3 (Aug. 1953): 326-340. BE, pp. 62-82. CP III, pp. 87-103. RI.

BOOK

The Organizational Revolution: A Study in the Ethics of Economic Organization. New York: Harper & Brothers, 1953. xxxiv + 286 pp. Translation: Japanese. Paperback edition: Quadrangle Books, 1968. xxxvi + 235 pp. Reissued: Westport, Conn.: Greenwood Press, 1984.

BOOK REVIEWS

Projection, Prediction, and Precariousness. Review article (with others) of Gerald Colm, The American Economy in 1960 (National Planning Association Staff Report). **Review of Economics and Statistics**, 35, 4 (Nov. 1953): 257-260. Correction and Apology. **Review of Economics and Statistics**, 36, 1 (Feb. 1954): 100.

Economic Theory and Measurement. Review of The Cowles Commission, Economic Theory and Measurement: Twenty Year Research Report, 1932-1952. **Kyklos**, 6, 2 (1953): 149-152.

Review of V.A. Demant, Religion and the Decline of Capitalism. **Journal of Religious Thought**, 10, 2 (Spring-Summer 1953): 180-181.

Review of Benjamin Higgins, What Do Economists Know? **Journal of Business**, 26, 2 (Apr. 1953): 139.

A Note on the Theory of Investment of the Firm. Review of Friedrich and Vera Lutz, The Theory of Investment of the Firm. **Kyklos**, 6, 1 (1953): 77-81.

1954

ARTICLES

Comment (on Vernon W. Malach, "Sales and Output Taxes"). **American Economic Review**, 44, 1 (Mar. 1954): 129.

An Economist's View of the Manpower Concept. In: **Proceedings of a Conference on the Utilization of Scientific and Professional Manpower** (National Manpower Council Conference, Arden House, Columbia University, Oct. 1953). New York: Columbia University Press, 1954, pp. 11-26; discussion, pp. 26-33. BE, pp. 12-27. CP I, pp. 417-432.

The Principle of Personal Responsibility. **Review of Social Economy**, 12, 1 (Mar. 1954): 1-8. BE, pp. 210-218. CP IV, pp. 11-20.

The Skills of the Economist (in Portuguese). **Revista Brasilerra de Economia**, 189 (Mar. 1954).

Twenty-Five Theses on Peace and Trade. **Friend**, 127 (Mar. 4, 1954): 290-292. CP V, pp. 23-27. RI.

BOOK REVIEWS

Projection, Prediction, and Precariousness: Correction and Apology. See: Book Reviews, 1953.

Review of Milton Friedman, Essays in Positive Economics. **Political Science Quarterly**, 69, 1 (Mar. 1954): 132-133.

The Concept of Property in Modern Christian Thought. Review of Frank Grace,
  The Concept of Property in Modern Christian Thought. **Michigan Alumnus
  Quarterly Review** (May 1954): 272-273.

Review of Kenneth D. Roose, The Economics of Recession and Revival. **Annals of
  the American Academy of Political and Social Science**, 296 (Nov. 1954): 178.

1955

ARTICLES

An Application of Population Analysis to the Automobile Population of the
  United States. **Kyklos,** 8, 2 (1955): 109-122. CP I, pp. 433-450.

Contributions of Economics to the Theory of Conflict. **Bulletin of the
  Research Exchange on the Prevention of War,** 3, 5 (May 1955): 51-59. CP V,
  pp. 29-39.

In Defense of Statics. **Quarterly Journal of Economics,** 69, 4 (Nov. 1955):
  485-502. CP I, pp. 465-484. RI.

The Malthusian Model as a General System. **Social and Economic Studies,** 4, 3
  (Sept. 1955): 195-205. CP I, pp. 451-463. RI.

Notes on the Information Concept. **Exploration** (Toronto), 6 (1955): 103-
  112. CP IV, pp. 21-32.

Parity, Charity, and Clarity: Ten Theses on Agricultural Policy. **Michigan
  Daily,** Oct. 16, 1955, p. 3. CP III, pp. 121-125.

Possible Conflicts Between Economic Stability and Economic Progress. **Farm
  Policy Forum,** 8, 1 (1955): 30-36.

BOOK

Economic Analysis. 3rd edition. New York: Harper & Brothers, 1955. xx +
  905 pp. Translations: Burmese, Japanese, Portuguese, Spanish, Turkish.
  See also: Books, 1941, 1948, 1966.

BOOK REVIEWS

Review of T. Haavelmo, A Study in the Theory of Economic Evolution:
  Contributions to Economic Analysis, III. **Kyklos,** 8, 1 (1955): 91-92.

Review of Albert Lauterbach, Man, Motives, and Money: Psychological Frontiers
  of Economics. **Social Order,** 5, 3 (1955): 135-136.

French Keynes. Review of Pierre Mendes-France and Gabriel Ardant, Economics
  and Action (UNESCO Publication). **Christian Century,** 72, 36 (Sept. 7,
  1955): 1024.

Review of Clarence B. Randall, Economics and Public Policy; and A Foreign Economic Policy for the United States. **Christian Century**, 72, 22 (June 1, 1955): 657-658.

VERSE

The Conservationist's Lament; The Technologist's Rely. **Population Bulletin** (Aug. 1955): 70. Also in: **Man's Role in Changing the Face of the Earth**, William L. Thomas, Jr., ed. (international symposium, Princeton, N.J., June 1955). Chicago: University of Chicago Press, for the Wenner-Gren Foundation for Anthropological Research and the National Science Foundation, 1956, p. 1087. RI.

1956

ARTICLES

Changes in Physical Phenomena: Discussion (with others). In: **Man's Role in Changing the Face of the Earth**, William L. Thomas, Jr., ed. (international symposium, Princeton, N.J., June 1955). Chicago: University of Chicago Press, for the Wenner-Gren Foundation for Anthropological Research and the National Science Foundation, 1956, pp. 917-929.

Commentary (Perspectives on Prosperity). **Social Action**, 22, 8 (Apr. 1956): 15-16.

Economics and the Behavioral Sciences: A Desert Frontier? **Diogenes**, 15 (Fall 1956): 1-14. CP III, pp. 105-120.

Economics: The Taming of Mammon. In: **Frontiers of Knowledge in the Study of Man**, Lynn White, Jr., ed. New York: Harper & Brothers, 1956, pp. 132-149. BE, pp. 26-42.

General Systems Theory: The Skeleton of Science. **Management Science**, 2, 3 (Apr. 1956): 197-208. BE, pp. 81-97. CP IV, pp. 33-46. RI.

Industrial Revolution and Urban Dominance: Discussion (with others). In: **Man's Role in Changing the Face of the Earth**, William L. Thomas, Jr., ed. (international symposium, Princeton, N.J., June 1955). Chicago: University of Chicago Press, for the Wenner-Gren Foundation for Anthropological Research and the National Science Foundation, 1956, pp. 434-448.

Limits of the Earth: Discussion (with others). In: **Man's Role in Changing the Face of the Earth**, William L. Thomas, Jr., ed. (international symposium, Princeton, N.J., June 1955). Chicago: University of Chicago Press, for the Wenner-Gren Foundation for Anthropological Research and the National Science Foundation, 1956, pp. 1071-1087.

Some Contributions of Economics to the General Theory of Value. **Philosophy of Science**, 23, 1 (Jan. 1956): 1-14. CP II, pp. 1-16. RI.

Statement Before the Subcommittee of the Senate Committee on Foreign Relations, U.S. Congress (on behalf of the Friends Committee on National

Legislation). In: **Control and Reductions of Armaments** (Hearing of the Committee). Washington, D.C.: U.S. Government Printing Office, 1956, Part 8, pp. 418-437.

Structure and Stability: The Economics of the Next Adjustment. In: **Policies to Combat Depression** (Conference of the Universities-National Bureau Committee for Economic Research). Princeton, N.J.: Princeton University Press, for the National Bureau of Economic Research, 1956, pp. 59-76. CP II, pp. 17-34.

BOOK

The Image: Knowledge in Life and Society. Ann Arbor: University of Michigan Press, 1956. 175 pp. Translations: German, Japanese. Paperback edition: Ann Arbor: University of Michigan Press, 1961. 184 pp.

BOOK REVIEWS

Review of J.T. Bonner, Cells and Societies. **American Anthropologist**, 58, 1 (Feb. 1956): 216.

Review of Neil W. Chamberlain, A General Theory of Economic Process. **Social Order**, 6, 3 (Mar. 1956): 128-130.

Ecumenical Social Thought. Review of Edward Duff, The Social Thought of the World Council of Churches. **Social Order**, 6, 8 (Oct. 1956): 392-397.

Review of C. Addison Hickman and Manford H. Kuhn, Individuals, Groups, and Economic Behavior. **Southern Economic Journal**, 23, 2 (Oct. 1956): 188-190.

Review of L.M. Lachmann, Capital and Its Structure. **American Economic Review**, 46, 5 (Dec. 1956): 988-989.

Warning to Ninevah. Review of Gunnar Myrdal, An International Economy: Problems and Prospects. **Christian Century**, 73, 37 (Sept. 12, 1956): 1053-1054.

1957

ARTICLES

Does the Absence of Monopoly Power in Agriculture Influence the Stability and Level of Farm Income? In: **Policy for Commercial Agriculture: Its Relation to Economic Growth and Stability** (papers submitted by panelists appearing before the Subcommittee on Agricultural Policy of the Joint Economic Committee, U.S. Congress). Washington, D.C.: U.S. Government Printing Office, 1957, pp. 42-50. CP II, pp. 111-121. RI.

Economic Theory: The Reconstruction Reconstructed. In: **Segments of the Economy -- 1956: A Symposium** (Economics-in-Action Program, Case Institute of Technology, Summer 1957). Cleveland, Ohio: Howard Allen, 1957, pp. 8-55. CP II, pp. 35-85.

A Look at the Corporation. In: **The Lamp** (75th Anniversary of Jersey Standard). New York: Standard Oil Company (N.J.), 1957, pp. 6-7.

A New Look at Institutionalism. **American Economic Review** (Papers and Proceedings of the 69th American Economic Association annual meeting, Cleveland, Dec. 1956), 47, 2 (May 1957): 1-12. CP II, pp. 87-100.

Organization and Conflict. **Journal of Conflict Resolution**, 1, 2 (June 1957): 122-134. RI.

Some Contributions of Economics to Theology and Religion. **Religious Education**, 52, 6 (Nov.-Dec. 1957): 446-450. BE, pp. 217-226. CP IV, pp. 47-53.

Some Reflections on Inflation and Economic Development. In: **Contribucôes à Análise do Desinvolvimento Econômico** (Festschrift in honor of Eugenio Gudin). Rio de Janeiro: Instituto Brasileiro dé Economia da Fundacão Getúlio Vargas, 1957, pp. 61-67. CP II, pp. 101-109.

BOOK REVIEWS

Review of Joe S. Bain, Barriers to New Competition: Their Character and Consequences in Manufacturing Industries. **Administrative Science Quarterly**, 2, 1 (June 1957): 116-118.

Review of John Maurice Clark, Economic Institutions and Human Welfare. **American Economic Review**, 47, 5 (Dec. 1957): 1004-1005.

Review of Lester de Koster, All Ye That Labor; An Essay on Christianity, Communism and the Problem of Evil. **Reformed Journal** (July-Aug. 1957): 20.

Review of Richard L. Meier, Science and Economic Development: New Patterns of Living. **American Journal of Sociology**, 63 (Sept. 1957): 240-242.

The Parsonian Approach to Economics. Review of Talcott Parsons and Neil J. Smelser, Economy and Society: A Study in the Integration of Economic and Social Theory. **Kyklos**, 10, 3 (1957): 317-319. RI.

1958

ARTICLES

The Current State of Economics. **Challenge**, 6, 10 (Aug.-Sept. 1958): 18-24.

Democracy and Organization. **Challenge**, 6, 6 (Mar. 1958): 13-17. CP V, pp. 41-47.

Evidences for an Administrative Science: A Review of the Administrative Science Quarterly, Volumes 1 and 2. **Administrative Science Quarterly**, 3, 1 (June 1958): 1-22. RI.

The Jungle of Hugeness: The Second Age of the Brontosaurus. **Saturday Review,** 41, 9 (Mar. 1, 1958): 11-13. CP II, pp. 123-131. RI.

"The Organization Man" -- Fact or Fancy? In: **The Emerging Environment of Industrial Relations.** East Lansing: Michigan State University, 1958, pp. 66-69.

Religion and the Social Sciences. In: **Religion and the State University,** Erich A. Walter, ed. Ann Arbor: University of Michigan Press, 1958, pp. 136-155. CP IV, pp. 55-76.

Secular Images of Man in the Social Sciences (paper presented at the National Convention of the Religious Education Association, Chicago, Nov. 1957). **Religious Education,** 53, 2 (Mar.-Apr. 1958): 91-96. CP IV, pp. 77-84. RI.

The Sputnik Within. **Liberation,** 2, 10 (Jan. 1958): 13-14.

Statement Before the Subcommittee on Agricultural Policy of the Joint Economic Committee, U.S. Congress. In: **Policy for Commercial Agriculture: Its Relation to Economic Growth and Stability** (Hearings of the Committee). Washington, D.C.: U.S. Government Printing Office, 1958, pp. 16-18.

Three Concepts of Disarmament. **American Friend** (special issue on Disarmament), NS 46, 4 (Feb. 20, 1958): 53-54.

Universal, Policed Disarmament as the Only Stable System of National Defense. In: **Problems of United States Economic Development.** New York: Committee for Economic Development, Jan. 1958, pp. 361-367.

BOOKS

Principles of Economic Policy. Englewood Cliffs, N.J.: Prentice-Hall, 1958. vi + 440 pp. Translations: Japanese, Portuguese, Spanish.

The Skills of the Economist. Cleveland, Ohio: Howard Allen, 1958. vi + 193 pp. Editions: British, Canadian. Translation: Japanese.

BOOK REVIEWS

Review article of Thomas C. Cochran, The American Business System: A Historical Perspective, 1900-1955 (with John Kenneth Galbraith). **Business History Review,** 32, 1 (Spring 1958): 116-121.

Review of Instituto Brasileiro dé Economia da Fundacão Getúlio Vargas, Contribuicões à Análise do Desinvolvimento Econômico (Festschrift in honor of Eugenio Gudin). **American Economic Review,** 48, 3 (June 1958): 462-463.

Theoretical Systems and Political Realities. Review of Morton A. Kaplan, System and Process in International Politics. **Journal of Conflict Resolution,** 2, 4 (Dec. 1958): 329-334.

Review of Erik Lundberg, Business Cycles and Economic Policy. **Annals of the American Academy of Political and Social Science,** 318 (July 1958): 179.

The Myth of the Ruling Class. Review of James H. Meisel, The Myth of the Ruling Class: Gaetano Mosca and the "Elite." **Michigan Alumnus Quarterly Review**, 65, 10 (Dec. 6, 1958): 88-89.

Groaning Table. Review of Wilbur Schramm, Responsibility in Mass Communication. **Christian Century**, 75, 9 (Feb. 26, 1958): 252.

VERSE

The Brandywine River Anthology (written for a seminar for educators sponsored by the Du Pont Company, Wilmington, Del., Mar. 1958). **Michigan Business Review**, 10, 2 (Mar. 1958): 7-9.

T.R. **Library of Congress Journal of Current Acquisitions** (15th Anniversary issue including "The Theodore Roosevelt Centennial Exhibit"), 15, 3 (May 1958): 100.

1959

ARTICLES

Foreword. In: **Population: The First Essay,** by T.R. Malthus. Ann Arbor, Mich.: Ann Arbor Paperbacks, 1959, pp. v-xii. CP II, pp. 133-142. RI.

The Knowledge of Value and the Value of Knowledge. In: **Ethics and the Social Sciences**, Leo R. Ward, ed. (lectures at Notre Dame, Fall 1957). Notre Dame, Ind.: Notre Dame University Press, 1959, pp. 25-42. CP IV, pp. 85-104.

National Images and International Systems (paper presented at the American Psychological Association meeting, Washington, D.C., Aug. 1958). **Journal of Conflict Resolution**, 3, 2 (June 1959): 120-131. CP V, pp. 49-62. RI.

Organizing Growth. **Challenge**, 8, 3 (Dec. 1959): 31-36. CP IV, pp. 105-112.

Symbols for Capitalism. **Harvard Business Review**, 37, 1 (Jan.-Feb. 1959): 41-48. CP II, pp. 143-152. RI.

BOOK REVIEWS

Review of Bernard Biet, Theories Contemporaines du Profit. **Econometrica**, 27, 2 (Apr. 1959): 321.

Review of Arthur H. Cole, Business Enterprise in Its Social Setting. **Administrative Science Quarterly**, 4, 3 (Dec. 1959): 361-362.

Review of John Kenneth Galbraith, The Affluent Society. **Review of Economics and Statistics**, 41, 1 (Feb. 1959): 81.

The Mighty Dollar. Review of F. Ernest Johnson and J. Emory Ackerman, The Church as Employer, Money Raiser and Investor. **Christian Century**, 76, 47 (Nov. 25, 1959): 1376-1377.

Review of John B. Rae, American Automobile Manufacturers: The First Forty Years. **Technology and Culture**, 1, 1 (Winter 1959): 104-105.

1960

ARTICLES

Capital and Interest. **Encyclopedia Britannica**, Vol. 4 (1960): 799-801. CP II, pp. 309-322. RI.

The Costs of Independence: Notes on the Caribbean. **Challenge**, 9, 3 (Dec. 1960): 14-18.

Decision-Making in the Modern World. In: **An Outline of Man's Knowledge of the Modern World**, Lyman Bryson, ed. New York: McGraw-Hill, 1960, pp. 410-442.

The Domestic Implications of Arms Control. **Daedalus** (special issue on Arms Control), 89, 4 (Fall 1960): 846-859. CP V, p. 63-78. RI.

The Present Position of the Theory of the Firm. In: **Linear Programming and the Theory of the Firm**, K.E. Boulding and W. Allen Spivey, eds. New York: Macmillan, 1960, pp. 1-17. CP II, pp. 153-171.

Scientific Nomenclature. **Science**, 131, 3404 (Mar. 18, 1960): 874, 876; **Science**, 131, 3412 (May 20, 1960): 1556-1567.

Standards for Our Economic System: Discussion (with others). **American Economic Review** (Papers and Proceedings of the 72nd American Economic Association annual meeting, Washington, D.C., Dec. 1959), 50, 2 (May 1960): 23-24.

A Theory of Small Society. **Caribbean Quarterly** (Jamaica), 6, 4 (1960): 258-269. CP IV, pp. 113-126.

Violence and Revolution: Some Reflections on Cuba. **Liberation**, 5, 2 (Apr. 1960): 5-8. RI.

BOOK

Linear Programming and the Theory of the Firm (edited with W. Allen Spivey). New York: Macmillan, 1960. x + 227 pp. Translation: French.

BOOK REVIEWS

Philosophy, Behavioral Science, and the Nature of Man. Review article of Hannah Arendt, The Human Condition; and Christian Bay, The Structure of Freedom. **World Politics**, 12, 2 (Jan. 1960): 272-279.

Review of Edward S. Mason, ed., The Corporation in Modern Society. **Business History Review**, 34, 4 (Winter 1960): 499-501.

Review of Reinhold Niebuhr, The Structure of Nations and Empires. **Review of Religious Research,** 1, 3 (Winter 1960): 122-124.

Review of Overton H. Taylor, The Classical Liberalism, Marxism, and the Twentieth Century. **American Economic Review,** 50, 1 (Mar. 1960): 168-169.

Review of Willard L. Thorp and Richard E. Quandt, The New Inflation. **Journal of the American Statistical Association,** 55, 291 (Sept. 1960): 616-617.

Review of Geoffrey Vickers, The Undirected Society: Essays on the Human Implications of Industrialisation in Canada. **Journal of Political Economy,** 68, 4 (Aug. 1960): 419-420.

1961

ARTICLES AND PAMPHLET

Contemporary Economic Research. In: **Trends in Social Science,** Donald P. Ray, ed. (presentations at the special symposium held by the Section on Social and Economic Sciences, American Association for the Advancement of Science annual meeting, Washington, D.C., 1958). New York: Philosophical Library, 1961, pp. 9-26.

The Dynamics of Disarmament. **Intercollegian,** 78, 8 (May 1961): 10-14.

Economic Resources and World Peace. In: **The Challenge of the '60s** (Lecture-Seminary Series 1960-61). Palo Alto, Calif.: Palo Alto Unified School District, 1961, pp. 27-35.

Our Attitude Toward Revolution. **Think,** 27, 7 (July-Aug. 1961): 27-29.

Perspective on the Economics of Peace (pamphlet). Part I of Economic Factors Bearing upon the Maintenance of Peace (Report to the Committee on Research for Peace). New York: Institute for International Order, 1961. 38 pp.

Political Implications of General Systems Research (presidential address to the Society for General Systems Research, American Association for the Advancement of Science annual meeting, Indianapolis, Dec. 1958). **General Systems Yearbook,** Vol. VI (1961): 1-7. CP IV, pp. 127-135.

The Public Image of American Economic Institutions. In: **American Perspectives: The National Self-Image in the Twentieth Century,** Robert E. Spiller and Eric Larrabee, eds. Cambridge, Mass.: Harvard University Press, 1961, pp. 117-133. CP III, pp. 127-145.

A Pure Theory of Conflict Applied to Organizations. In: **Conflict Management in Organizations** (report of a seminar conducted by the Foundation in cooperation with the Center for Research on Conflict Resolution, University of Michigan, Oct. 1961). Ann Arbor, Mich.: Foundation for Research on Human Behavior, 1961, pp. 43-51. CP V, pp. 79-89. RI.

Reflections on Poverty. In: **The Social Welfare Forum, 1961** (Proceedings of the 88th Annual Forum, Minneapolis, May 1961). New York: Columbia

University Press, for the National Conference on Social Welfare, 1961, pp. 45-58. CP II, pp. 181-196.

Social Dynamics in West Indian Society. **Social and Economic Studies**, 10, 1 (Mar. 1961): 25-34.

Some Difficulties in the Concept of Economic Input. In: **Output, Input, and Productivity Measurement** (Studies in Income and Wealth, Vol. 25; National Bureau of Economic Research conference, Carnegie Endowment International Center, New York, Oct. 1958). Princeton, N.J.: Princeton University Press, 1961, pp. 331-345. CP II, pp. 197-208.

Study of the Soviet Economy: Its Place in American Education (discussion with others). In: **Study of the Soviet Economy**, Nicolas Spulber, ed. (Russian and East European Series, Vol. 25). Bloomington: Indiana University Publications, 1961, pp. 104-128.

The U.S. and Revolution (with others). In: **The U.S. and Revolution** (An Occasional Paper on the Free Society). Santa Barbara, Calif.: Center for the Study of Democratic Institutions, 1961, pp. 4-7. CP V, pp. 91-96. RI.

What is Economic Progress? (in French). **Cahiers de l'Institut de Science Économique Appliquée** (Paris), 110 (Feb. 1961): 147-155. CP II (in English), pp. 173-180.

Where Do We Go From Here, If Anywhere? In: **Proceedings of the Fourteenth National Conference on the Administration of Research** (University of Michigan, Sept. 1960). University Park: Pennsylvania State University Press, 1961, pp. 66-72. CP II, pp. 209-217.

BOOK REVIEWS

French Window. Review of Raymond Aron, Introduction to the Philosophy of History. **Christian Century**, 78, 33 (Aug. 16, 1961): 981.

Review of Jean Fourastié, The Causes of Wealth, translated by Theodore Caplow, **Technology and Culture**, 2, 3 (Summer 1961): 262-264.

Trying to Square the Circle. Review of Charles J. Hitch and Roland McKean, The Economics of Defense in the Nuclear Age. **Bulletin of the Atomic Scientists**, 17, 3 (Mar. 1961): 115-116.

Nothing Rash. Review of P.B. Medawar, The Future of Man: Predictions of a Biologist. **Christian Century**, 78, 20 (May 17, 1961): 623.

Review of Gunnar Myrdal, Beyond the Welfare State: Economic Planning and Its International Implications. **Administrative Science Quarterly**, 6, 1 (June 1961): 107-109.

Review of Talcott Parsons, Structure and Process in Modern Societies. **Psychiatry**, 24, 3 (Aug. 1961): 278-279.

The Nightmare of Rationality. Review of Thomas C. Schelling, The Strategy of Conflict. **Contemporary Psychology**, 8, 2 (June 1961): 426-427.

Review of Dan Wilson, An Opening Way (Pendle Hill Pamphlet No. 113). **Quaker Life**, 2, 7 (July 1961): 189.

VERSE

A Shelter for All (Preamble to a Statement issued by the Friends National Conference on World Order, Richmond, Ind., Oct. 1961). **Friends Journal**, 7, 23 (Dec. 1, 1961): 489.

1962

ARTICLES

Better R-E-D than Dead. **New Republic** (special issue on Time for a Keynes: An Inquiry into What New Economic Thinking Is Required for the U.S. in the Sixties), 147, 16 (Oct. 20, 1962): 15-16. RI.

Can We Afford a Warless World? **Saturday Review**, 45, 40 (Oct. 6, 1962): 17-20. RI.

Economics and Accounting: The Uncongenial Twins. In: **Studies in Accounting Theory**, W.T. Baxter and Sidney Davidson, eds. London: Sweet and Maxwell, 1962, pp. 44-55. CP II, pp. 219-232. RI.

The Ethical Perspective. In: **Christians Face Issues of High Moment in Our Changing Economy** (papers for the National Study Conference on the Church and Economic Life, Pittsburgh, Nov. 1962). New York: National Council of Churches, 1962, pp. 35-44. CP IV, pp. 137-148. RI.

Ethics and Business: An Economist's View (presentation at a seminar, Pennsylvania State University, Mar. 1962). In: **Ethics and Business.** University Park: Pennsylvania State University, College of Business Administration, Sept. 1962, pp. 1-14. BE, pp. 225-238. RI.

An Interdisciplinary Honors Course in General Systems. **Superior Student** (Boulder, Colo.), 4, 7 (Jan.-Feb. 1962): 31.

Is Peace Researchable? **Continuous Learning** (Toronto), 1, 2 (Mar.-Apr. 1962): 63-69. CP V, pp. 97-105. RI.

Knowledge as a Commodity (presentation at a special session co-sponsored by the American Economic Association, American Association for the Advancement of Science annual meeting, Denver, 1961). In: **Series Studies in Social and Economic Sciences** (Symposia Studies No. 11). Washington, D.C.: National Institute of Social and Behavioral Science, June 1962, pp. 1-6. BE, pp. 139-150.

Notes on a Theory of Philanthropy. In: **Philanthropy and Public Policy**, F.G. Dickinson, ed. (NBER Conference on Philanthropy, Merrill Center for Economics, Long Island, N.Y., June 1961). New York: National Bureau of Economic Research, 1962, pp. 57-71. CP II, pp. 233-249.

The Peace Research Movement. **Council for Correspondence Newsletter** (1962): 25-32. RI.

The Prevention of World War III. **Virginia Quarterly Review**, 38, 1 (Winter 1962): 1-12. CP V, pp. 107-119. RI.

A Pure Theory of Death: Dilemmas of Defense Policy in a World of Conditional Viability. In: **Behavioral Science and Civil Defense**, George W. Baker and Leonard S. Cottrell, Jr., eds. (presentations at the conference on Behavioral Science and Civil Defense, Washington, D.C., May 1961; National Academy of Sciences-National Research Council Publication No. 997). Washington, D.C.: National Academy of Sciences, 1962, pp. 53-69. BE, pp. 112-130.

The Relations of Economic, Political and Social Systems. **Social and Economic Studies** (special issue on the Conference on Political Sociology in the British Caribbean, Jamaica, Dec. 1961), 11, 4 (Dec. 1962): 351-362. BE, pp. 96-111. CP IV, pp. 149-162.

The Role of the Price Structure in Economic Development (with Pritam Singh). **American Economic Review** (Papers and Proceedings of the 74th American Economic Association annual meeting, New York, Dec. 1961), 52, 2 (May 1962): 28-38. CP II, pp. 251-263.

Social Justice in Social Dynamics. In: **Social Justice**, Richard B. Brandt, ed. (based on lectures presented under the auspices of the William J. Cooper Foundation, Swarthmore College, Spring 1961). New York: Prentice-Hall, 1962, pp. 73-92. BE, pp. 239-257. CP IV, pp. 163-184.

Some Questions on the Measurement and Evaluation of Organization. In: **Ethics and Bigness: Scientific, Academic, Religious, Political, and Military**, Harlan Cleveland and Harold D. Lasswell, eds. (papers prepared for the 16th meeting of the Conference on Science, Philosophy and Religion in Their Relation to the Democratic Way of Life, Jewish Theological Seminary of America, New York, Aug. 1960). New York: Harper & Brothers, 1962, pp. 385-395. BE, pp. 129-140. CP III, pp. 147-159.

War as an Economic Institution. In: **The Causes of War** (Final Report of the 3rd Annual Seminar on International Affairs, Nov. 1961). Montreal: Sir George Williams University, 1962, pp. 38-48.

Where Are We Going, If Anywhere? A Look at Post-Civilization. **Human Organization** (special issue on Major Issues in Modern Society), 21, 2 (Summer 1962): 162-167. RI.

BOOK

Conflict and Defense: A General Theory. New York: Harper & Brothers, 1962. ix + 343 pp. Translation: Japanese. Paperback edition: New York: Harper & Brothers, 1963. ix + 349 pp.

BOOK REVIEWS

Review of John Maurice Clark, Competition as a Dynamic Process. **Annals of the American Academy of Political and Social Science**, 343 (Sept. 1962): 181-182.

Political Non-Science. Review of Marshall E. Dimock, The New American Political Economy; and C.E. Ayres, Toward a Reasonable Society. **Science,** 136, 3515 (May 11, 1962): 509-510.

An Economist's View. Review of George Caspar Homans, Social Behavior: Its Elementary Forms. **American Journal of Sociology,** 67, 4 (Jan. 1962): 458-461.

Pacifists, Too, Must Think. Review article of Herman Kahn, Thinking About the Unthinkable. **Fellowship,** 28, 14 (Sept. 1, 1962): 27-30.

Review of Gardiner C. Means, Pricing Power and the Public Interest: A Study Based on Steel. **Administrative Science Quarterly,** 7, 2 (Sept. 1962): 266-268.

Review of Fred L. Polak, The Image of the Future, Vols. I and II, translated from the Dutch by Elise Boulding. **Journal of Political Economy,** 70, 2 (Apr. 1962): 192-193.

Review of Kurt Samuelsson, Religion and Economic Action, translated from the Swedish by E. Geoffrey French. **Journal of Political Economy,** 70, 4 (Aug. 1962): 423-424.

Review of Allen M. Sievers, Revolution, Evolution and the Economic Order. **Journal of Finance,** 17, 4 (Dec. 1962): 705-706.

VERSE

Some Reflections. In: **The Church in a World That Won't Hold Still** (report of the 4th National Study Conference on the Church and Economic Life, Pittsburgh, Nov. 1962). New York: National Council of Churches, 1962, p. 48.

1963

ARTICLES

Agricultural Organizations and Policies: A Personal Evaluation. In: **Farm Goals in Conflict: Farm Family Income, Freedom, Security** (presentations at the Second Conference on Goals and Values in Agriculture, sponsored by the Center for Agricultural and Economic Development, Feb. 1963). Ames: Iowa State University Press, 1963, pp. 156-166. CP III, pp. 161-173.

The Death of the City: A Frightened Look at Post-Civilization. In: **The Historian and the City,** Oscar Handlin and John Burchard, eds. (papers presented at the Conference on the City and History, Harvard Summer School, Cambridge, July 1961). Cambridge, Mass.: M.I.T. Press, 1963, pp. 133-145. CP II, pp. 265-279.

The Future Corporation and Public Attitudes. In: **The Corporation and Its Publics; Essays on the Corporate Image,** John W. Riley, Jr. ed. (papers prepared for the Foundation for Research on Human Behavior Symposium, Gould

House, Ardsley-on-Hudson, N.Y., Spring 1961). New York: John Wiley & Sons, 1963, pp. 159-175. CP III, pp. 175-193.

The Misallocation of Intellectual Resources. **Proceedings of the American Philosophical Society,** 107, 2 (Apr. 1963): 117-120. BE, pp. 149-157. CP III, pp. 195-200.

Pacem in Terris and the World Community (with others; comments on the Pope's Encyclical). **Continuum,** 1, 2 (Summer 1963): 214-217.

Preface (with Emile Benoit). In: **Disarmament and the Economy,** Emile Benoit and Kenneth Boulding, eds. New York: Harper & Row, 1963, pp. vii-x.

The Role of Law in the Learning of Peace. **Proceedings of the American Society of International Law** (1963): 92-103. CP V, pp. 121-134.

The Society of Abundance. In: **The Church in a Society of Abundance,** Arthur E. Walmsley, ed. New York: Seabury Press, 1963, pp. 9-27. CP IV, pp. 185-205.

Towards a Pure Theory of Threat Systems. **American Economic Review** (Papers and Proceedings of the 75th American Economic Association annual meeting, Pittsburgh, Dec. 1962), 53, 2 (May 1963): 424-434. CP V, pp. 135-147. RI.

The University, Society and Arms Control. **Journal of Conflict Resolution,** 7, 3 (Sept. 1963): 458-463; **Journal of Arms Control** (joint volume; Proceedings of the International Arms Control Symposium, Ann Arbor, Mich., Dec. 1962), 1, 4 (Oct. 1963): 552-557.

The Uses of Price Theory. In: **Models of Markets,** Alfred R. Oxenfeldt, ed. (papers presented at the Conference on Appraisals of the Market Models of Price Theory, Arden House, Harriman, N.Y., Apr. 1962, and a later conference). New York: Columbia University Press, 1963, pp. 146-162. CP II, pp. 281-299.

The World War Industry as an Economic Problem. In: **Disarmament and the Economy,** Emile Benoit and Kenneth Boulding, eds. New York: Harper & Row, 1963, pp. 3-27.

BOOK

Disarmament and the Economy (edited with Emile Benoit; final report of the Program of Research on Economic Adjustments to Disarmament, READ, sponsored by the Center for Research on Conflict Resolution, University of Michigan). New York: Harper & Row, 1963. 310 pp. Reissued: Westport, Conn.: Greenwood Press, 1978.

BOOK REVIEWS

Two Recent Studies of Modern Society. Review of Sebastian de Grazia, Of Time, Work, and Leisure; and Hugh Dalziel Duncan, Communication and Social Order. **Scientific American,** 208, 1 (Jan. 1963): 157-160.

Review of Milton Friedman, Capitalism and Freedom. **Journal of Business,** 36, 1 (Jan. 1963): 120-121.

Review of Klaus Knorr and Sidney Verba, eds., The International System: Theoretical Essays. **American Journal of Sociology,** 68 (1962-63): 380-381.

The Knowledge Industry. Review of Fritz Machlup, The Production and Distribution of Knowledge in the United States. **Challenge,** 11, 8 (May 1963): 36-38.

Review of Victor Perlo, Militarism and Industry -- Arms Profiteering in the Missile Age. **American Economic Review,** 53, 4 (Sept. 1963): 809-810.

Review of Joan Robinson, Economic Philosophy. **American Sociological Review,** 28, 4 (Aug. 1963): 657-658.

Review of W. Lloyd Warner, The Corporation in the Emergent American Society. **American Journal of Sociology,** 68, 6 (May 1963): 702.

Review of Quincy Wright, William M. Evan, and Morton Deutsch, eds., Preventing World War III: Some Proposals. **Annals of the American Academy of Political and Social Science,** 348 (July 1963): 225-226.

VERSE

Arden House Poetry. In: **Models of Markets,** Alfred R. Oxenfeldt, ed. (presentations at the Conference on Appraisal of the Market Models of Price Theory, Arden House, Harriman, N.Y., Apr. 1962, and a later conference). New York: Columbia University Press, 1963, pp. 369-371.

1964

ARTICLES AND PAMPHLET

The Dimensions of Economic Freedom. In: **The Nation's Economic Objectives,** Edgar O. Edwards, ed. (lectures presented during Rice University's 50th Anniversary, Houston, Spring 1963). Chicago: University of Chicago Press, 1964, pp. 107-122. BE, pp. 256-274. CP III, pp. 201-218. RI.

The Economist and the Engineer: Economic Dynamics of Water Resource Development. In: **Economics and Public Policy in Water Resource Development.** Stephen C. Smith and Emery N. Castle, eds. (papers presented to the Committee on the Economics of Water Resources Development of the Western Agricultural Economics Research Council). Ames: Iowa State University Press, 1964, pp. 82-92. CP III, pp. 219-231.

The Evolutionary Potential of Quakerism (Pendle Hill Pamphlet No. 136). Wallingford, Pa.: Pendle Hill, 1964. 31 pp.

General Systems as a Point of View. In: **Views on General Systems Theory,** Mihajlo D. Mesarovic, ed. (Proceedings of the Second Systems Symposium, Case Institute of Technology, Cleveland, Apr. 1963). New York: John Wiley & Sons, 1964, pp. 25-38. CP IV, pp. 207-222. RI.

Knowledge as an Economic Variable (paper presented at the Japanese Association of Theoretical Economics meeting, Tokyo, Fall 1963). **Economic Studies Quarterly** (Tokyo), 14, 3 (June 1964): 1-6. CP II, pp. 301-308.

Market: Economic Theory. **Encyclopedia Britannica**, Vol. 14 (1964): 913-914.

The Need for a Study on the Psychology of Disarmament. **Our Generation Against Nuclear War** (Supplement on Peace Research), 3, 2 (Oct. 1964): 39-41.

Needs and Opportunities in Peace Research and Peace Education. **Our Generation Against Nuclear War** (Supplement on Peace Research), 3, 2 (Oct. 1964): 22-25. CP V, pp. 149-154.

The Place of the Image in the Dynamics of Society (based on an address before the Public Relations Institute, Cornell University, Aug. 1961). In: **Explorations in Social Change,** George K. Zollschan and Walter Hirsch, eds. Boston: Houghton-Mifflin and London: Routledge and Kegan Paul, 1964, pp. 5-16. CP IV, pp. 223-236. RI.

The Possibilities of Peace Research in Australia. **Australian Outlook** (Melbourne), 18, 2 (Aug. 1964): 165-169.

Realism and Sentimentalism in the Student Movement. **ICU** (International Christian University, Tokyo), 11 (1963/64): 74-75.

Toward a Theory of Peace. In: **International Conflict and Behavioral Science -- The Craigville Papers,** Roger Fisher, ed. (papers prepared for the American Academy of Arts and Sciences Institute on Behavioral Science Research Toward Peace, Craigville, Mass., Aug. 1962). New York: Basic Books, 1964, pp. 70-87.

Two Principles of Conflict. In: **Power and Conflict in Organizations,** Robert L. Kahn and Elise Boulding, eds. (based on two seminars conducted by the Foundation for Research on Human Behavior, 1960 and 1961). New York: Basic Books, for the Foundation for Research on Human Behavior, Ann Arbor, Mich., 1964, pp. 75-76.

Why Did Gandhi Fail? In: **Gandhi -- His Relevance for Our Times,** G. Ramachandran and T.K. Mahadevan, eds. Bombay: Bharatiya Vidya Bhavan, for the Gandhi Peace Foundation, 1964, pp. 129-134. CP V, pp. 155-162. RI.

BOOK

The Meaning of the Twentieth Century: The Great Transition (Vol. 34 of the World Perspective Series, planned and edited by Ruth Nanda Anshen). New York: Harper & Row, 1964. xvi + 199 pp. Edition: British. Translations: Italian, Japanese, Portuguese, Spanish. Paperback edition: New York: Harper Colophon Books, 1965. 208 pp.

BOOK REVIEWS

Review of David Braybrooke and Charles E. Lindblom, A Strategy of Decision: Policy Evaluation as a Social Process. **American Sociological Review**, 29, 6 (Dec. 1964): 930-931.

Review of Richard M. Cyert and James G. March, A Behavioral Theory of the Firm. **American Sociological Review**, 29, 4 (Aug. 1964): 592-593.

The Content of International Studies in College: A Review. Review article of Ernst B. Haas and Allen S. Whiting, Dynamics of International Relations; Charles A. McClelland, College Teaching of International Relations; Hans J. Morgenthau, Politics Among Nations; A.F.K. Organski, World Politics; Norman Padelford and George A. Lincoln, The Dynamics of International Politics; James Rosenau, ed., International Politics and Foreign Policy: A Reader in Research and Theory; Charles P. Schleicher, International Relations; and John G. Stoessinger, The Might of Nations. **Journal of Conflict Resolution**, 8, 1 (Mar. 1964): 65-71.

Review of Alfred Kuhn, The Study of Society: A Unified Approach. **Accounting Review**, 39, 2 (Apr. 1964): 530-531.

Review of La Paix, Recueils de la Société Jean Bodin, pour L'Histoire Comparative. Editions de la Librarie Encyclopédique. **Comparative Studies in Society and History**, 6, 2 (Jan. 1964): 217-219.

Word Meanings in Economics. Review of Fritz Machlup, Essays on Economic Semantics, Merton H. Miller, Walter D. Fackler, and Tom E. Davis, eds. **Monthly Labor Review**, 87, 5 (May 1964): 577.

Statistical Image. Review of Angus Maddison, Economic Growth in the West: Comparative Experience in Europe and North America. **Science**, 146, 3648 (Nov. 27, 1964): 1151-1152.

Ice Enveloped in Fire. Review of Anatol Rapoport, Strategy and Conscience. **Peace News** (London), 1480 (Nov. 6, 1964): 8.

VERSE

Summaries (of papers presented). In: **Views on General Systems Theory**, Mihajlo D. Mesarovic, ed. (Proceedings of the Second Systems Symposium, Case Institute of Technology, Cleveland, Apr. 1963). New York: John Wiley & Sons, 1964, pp. 1, 25, 39, 61, 119, 125, 143.

1965

ARTICLES

America's Great Delusion. **Labor Today**, 4, 3 (June-July 1965): 21, 23.

The Changing Framework of American Capitalism. **Challenge**, 14, 2 (Nov.-Dec. 1965): 39-42. CP III, pp. 251-256.

The Communication of Legitimacy. **Channels** (Western Michigan University) (Spring 1965): 24-28. CP IV, pp. 237-243. RI.

The Concept of World Interest. In: **Economics and the Idea of Mankind**, Bert F. Hoselitz, ed. (under the auspices of the Council for the Study of Mankind). New York: Columbia University Press, 1965, pp. 41-62. RI.

The Difficult Art of Doing Good (lecture in the 1964 Summer Lecture Series, University of Colorado). **Colorado Quarterly,** 13, 3 (Winter 1965): 197-211. CP IV, pp. 245-261.

The Dilemma of Power and Legitimacy. In: **Power and Responsibility, Proceedings of the Institute of World Affairs** (Pasadena, Calif., Dec. 1964), Vol. 40. Los Angeles: University of Southern California, 1965, pp. 183-188. RI.

Economic Libertarianism. In: **Conference on Savings and Residential Financing, 1965 Proceedings.** Chicago: U.S. Savings and Loan League, Sept. 1965, pp. 30-42; discussion, pp. 42-57. BE, pp. 41-54. CP II, pp. 345-358.

Economics. In: **System Engineering Handbook,** Robert E. Machol, ed. New York: McGraw-Hill, 1965, pp. 35-1 to 35-8.

The Economics of Human Conflict. In: **The Nature of Human Conflict,** Elton B. McNeil, ed. Englewood Cliffs, N.J.: Prentice-Hall, 1965, pp. 172-191. CP II, pp. 323-344.

The Future of the Social Sciences. **Science Journal** (London), 1, 7 (Sept. 1965): 3.

Great Society, or Grandiose? **Washington Post,** Dec. 5, 1965, p. E3. RI.

How Scientists Study "Getting Along." In: **Our Working World: Neighbors at Work, Teacher's Resource Unit.** Chicago: Science Research Associates, 1965.

Insight and Knowledge in the Development of Stable Peace. In: **No Time But This Present, Studies Preparatory to the Fourth World Conference of Friends 1967.** Birmingham, Eng.: Friends World Committee for Consultation, 1965, pp. 210-219.

Looking Ahead to the Year 2000. **Fellowship,** 31, 5 (May 1965): 26-29.

The Menace of Methuselah: Possible Consequences of Increased Life Expectancy (address before the Washington Academy of Sciences, Mar. 1965). **Journal of the Washington Academy of Sciences,** 55, 7 (Oct. 1965): 171-179. CP IV, pp. 263-273.

Population and Poverty. **Correspondent,** 35 (Autumn 1965): 38-40. CP II, pp. 359-363. RI.

Reality Testing and Value Orientation in International Systems: The Role of Research (paper presented at the 6th International Studies Association annual meeting, Colorado Springs, Colo., Apr. 1965). **International Social Science Journal,** 17, 3 (Apr. 1965): 404-416; French translation: 432-445. RI.

Reflections on Protest. **Bulletin of the Atomic Scientists,** 21, 8 (Oct. 1965): 18-20. CP V, pp. 173-178. RI.

Research and Development for the Emergent Nations. In: **Economics of Research and Development,** Richard A. Tybout, ed. (OSU Conference on Economics of Research and Development, Oct. 1962). Columbus: Ohio State University Press, for the Mershon Center for Education in National Security, 1965, pp. 422-437; comments, 438-447. CP III, pp. 233-250.

Social Sciences. In: **The Great Ideas Today,** R.M. Hutchins and M.J. Adler, eds. Chicago: Encyclopedia Britannica, 1965, pp. 254-285. CP IV, pp. 275-306.

Statement Before the Subcommittee on Fiscal Policy of the Joint Economic Committee, U.S. Congress. In: **Fiscal Policy Issues of the Coming Decade** (materials submitted to the committee). Washington, D.C.: U.S. Government Printing Office, 1965, pp. 17-18.

War as a Public Health Problem: Conflict Management as a Key to Survival. In: **Behavioral Science and Human Survival,** Milton Schwebel, ed. (based on presentations at the American Orthopsychiatric Association annual meeting, Washington, D.C., Mar. 1963). Palo Alto, Calif.: Science and Behavioral Books, 1965, pp. 103-110. CP V, pp. 163-172. RI.

War as an Investment: The Strange Case of Japan (with Alan H. Gleason). **Peace Research Society (International) Papers** (Chicago Conference, 1964), Vol. III (1965): 1-17. CP III, pp. 257-275. RI.

BOOK REVIEWS

Review of David T. Bazelon, The Paper Economy. **Administrative Science Quarterly,** 9, 4 (Mar. 1965): 450-451.

Review of Karl De Schweinitz, Jr., Industrialization and Democracy: Economic Necessities and Political Possibilities. **American Economic Review,** 15, 1 (Mar. 1965): 181-182.

Is Economics Obsolescent? Review of Adolph Lowe, On Economic Knowledge: Toward a Science of Political Economics. **Scientific American,** 212, 5 (May 1965): 139-143.

The Medium and the Message. Review of Marshall McLuhan, The Gutenberg Galaxy: The Making of Typographic Man; and Understanding Media, The Extensions of Man. **Canadian Journal of Economics and Political Science,** 31, 2 (May 1965): 268-273. CP IV, pp. 307-314. RI.

Scabbard or Sword? Review of Walter Millis, An End To Arms (Center for the Study of Democratic Institutions Book); and Thomas S. Power with Albert A. Arnhym, Design for Survival. **Book Week,** May 2, 1965, pp. 15, 17.

1966

ARTICLES AND PAMPHLET

Arms Limitation and Integrative Activity as Elements in the Establishment of Stable Peace. **Peace Research Society (International) Papers** (Vienna Conference, 1966), Vol. VI (1966): 1-10. Slightly modified version in: **Arms Control for the Late Sixties,** James E. Dougherty and J.F. Lehman, eds. (presentations at the Third International Arms Control Symposium, Philadelphia, Apr. 1966). Princeton, N.J.: D. Van Nostrand, 1967, pp. 237-246.

The Concept of Need for Health Services (one of a series of papers on Health Services Research sponsored by the HSR Study Section of the U.S. Public Health Services). **Milbank Memorial Fund Quarterly**, Part 2, 44, 4 (Oct. 1966): 202-225. CP III, pp. 277-298. RI.

Conflict Management as a Learning Process. In: **Ciba Foundation Symposium on Conflict in Society**, Anthony de Reuck and Julie Knight, eds. (symposium at the Ciba Foundation, London, June 1965). London: J. & A. Churchill, 1966, pp. 236-248; discussion, pp. 249-258. CP V, pp. 179-183.

Economics and Ecology. In: **Future Environments in North America**, F. Fraser Darling and John P. Milton, eds. (Conservation Foundation conference, Airlie House, Warrenton, Va., Apr. 1965). Garden City, N.Y.: Natural History Press, 1966, pp. 225-234. CP III, pp. 299-310.

The Economics of Knowledge and the Knowledge of Economics (Richard T. Ely Lecture). **American Economic Review** (Papers and Proceedings of the 78th American Economic Association annual meeting, New York, Dec. 1965), 56, 2 (May 1966): 1-13. CP II, pp. 365-379. RI.

The Economics of the Coming Spaceship Earth. In: **Environmental Quality in a Growing Economy, Essays from the Sixth RFF Forum**, Henry Jarrett, ed. Baltimore, Md.: Johns Hopkins Press, for Resources for the Future, 1966, pp. 3-14. BE, pp. 273-287. CP II, pp. 381-394. RI.

The Ethics of Rational Decision (presentation at the 27th Operation Research Society of America national meeting, Boston, May 1965). **Management Science**, 12, 6 (Feb. 1966): B-161 to B-169. CP IV, pp. 315-325. RI.

Expecting the Unexpected: The Uncertain Future of Knowledge and Technology. In: **Perspective Changes in Society by 1980, Including Some Implications for Education**, Edgar L. Morphet and Charles O. Ryan, eds. (papers prepared for the First Area Conference, Denver, June 1966). Denver, Colo.: Designing Education for the Future, July 1966, pp. 199-215. BE, pp. 156-175. CP IV, pp. 327-343. RI.

Impressions of the World Conference on Church and Society (World Council of Churches Ecumenical Center, Geneva, Switz.). **Quaker Life**, 7, 9 (Sept. 1966): 287-289.

Integrative Aspects of the International System. In: **Proceedings of the International Peace Research Association Inaugural Conference**, H.J. Prakke and H.M.G. Prakke, eds. Assen, The Netherlands: Van Gorcum, 1966, pp. 27-38.

Is Scarcity Dead? **Public Interest**, 5 (Fall 1966): 36-44. CP III, pp. 311-321. RI.

The Knowledge Boom. **Challenge**, 14, 6 (July-Aug. 1966): 5-7.

Notes on the Politics of Peace. **Bulletin of the Atomic Scientists**, 22, 7 (Sept. 1966): 30-32.

The Parameters of Politics (Edmund J. James Lecture on Government, Apr. 1966). Urbana: **University of Illinois Bulletin**, 63, 139 (July 15, 1966): 1-21. CP V, pp. 195-215.

The Peculiar Economics of Water. **Chemistry**, 39, 9 (Sept. 1966): 20-21.

The Political Consequences of the Social Sciences (First Annual Political Awards Dinner Lecture, Dec. 1965; pamphlet). Kalamazoo: Michigan Center for Education in Politics, Western Michigan University, 1966. 13 pp.

A Profile of the American Economy. **America Illustrated** (in Russian), 10, 120 (1966): 10-13; (in Polish), 10, 93 (1966): 8-11; (in English; pamphlet) (1968). 4 pp.

Quakerism in the World of the Future (summary of Carey Memorial Lecture, Baltimore Yearly Meeting, Summer 1965). **Friends Journal** 12, 2 (Jan. 15, 1966): 29-31. RI.

The Role of the Museum in the Propagation of Developed Images. **Technology and Culture**, 7, 1 (Winter 1966): 64-66.

The Spotted Reality: The Fragmentation, Isolation and Conflict in Today's World. In: **1966 Current Issues in Higher Education: Higher Education Reflects--On Itself and on the Larger Society**, G. Kerry Smith, Tom Erhard, and Carol MacGuineas, eds. (Proceedings of the 21st Annual National Conference on Higher Education, Mar. 1966). Washington, D.C.: Association for Higher Education, 1966, pp. 7-16. RI.

Towards the Development of a Security Community in Europe. **Proceedings of the Sixteenth Pugwash Conference on Science and World Affairs, Sopot, Poland,** Vol. V (Sept. 1966): 122-130.

Verifiability of Economic Images. In: **The Structure of Economic Science: Essays on Methodology,** Sherman Krupp, ed. Englewood Cliffs, N.J.: Prentice-Hall, 1966, pp. 129-141. CP III, pp. 323-337.

The Wisdom of Man and the Wisdom of God. In: **Human Values on the Spaceship Earth.** New York: Council Press, for the Commission on Church and Economic Life of the National Council of Churches, 1966, pp. 1-33.

BOOKS

Economic Analysis. 4th edition; two volumes. New York: Harper & Row, 1966. Vol. I: Microanalysis. xxiv + 720 pp. Vol. II: Macroanalysis. xviii + 280 pp. Edition: Indian. Translations: Japanese, Spanish. See also: Books, 1941, 1948, 1955.

The Impact of the Social Sciences. New Brunswick, N.J.: Rutgers University Press, 1966. vi + 117 pp. Edition: Indian. Translations: Arabic, French, Japanese, Korean, Portuguese, Spanish.

BOOK REVIEWS

Review of Kalman J. Cohen and Richard M. Cyert, Theory of the Firm: Resource Allocation in a Market Economy. **Econometrica**, 34, 4 (Oct. 1966): 902-903.

Review of James S. Coleman, Introduction to Mathematical Sociology. **American Sociological Review**, 31, 1 (Feb. 1966): 131-132.

Review of Fred Charles Iklé, How Nations Negotiate. **American Journal of Sociology**, 71, 5 (Mar. 1966): 601-602.

Review of Oskar Lange, Wholes and Parts: A General Theory of System Behavior, translated from the Polish by Eugenius Lepa. **Econometrica**, 34, 2 (Apr. 1966): 510.

Space, Technology, and Society: From Puff-Puff to Whoosh. Review of Bruce Mazlish, ed., The Railroad and the Space Program: An Exploration in Historical Analogy. **Science**, 151, 3713 (Feb. 25, 1966): 979.

Review of Robert K. Merton, On the Shoulders of Giants; A Shandean Postscript. **American Sociological Review**, 31, 1 (Feb. 1966): 104-105.

Knowledge v. Wisdom in the Relation Between Scientists and the Government. Review of Don K. Price, The Scientific Estate. **Scientific American**, 214, 4 (Apr. 1966): 131-134.

Review of Anatol Rapoport and Albert Chammah, Prisoner's Dilemma: A Study in Conflict and Cooperation. **Michigan Daily**, Feb. 2, 1966, p. 4. Also: **Michigan Quarterly Review**, 6, 2 (Spring 1967): 142-144.

A "Space Ship" That May Explode. Review of Barbara Ward, Space Ship Earth. **Fellowship**, 32, 9 (Sept. 1966): 29.

Review of E.G. West, Education and the State: A Study in Political Economy. **University of Chicago Law Review**, 33, 3 (Spring 1966): 615-618.

VERSE

The Feather River Anthology. **Industrial Water Engineering**, 3, 12 (Dec. 1966): 32-33. RI.

Summary (of The Range of Human Conflict: A Symposium; American Psychiatric Association meeting, May 1965). **Bulletin of the Menninger Clinic**, 30, 5 (Sept. 1966): 313-314.

1967

ARTICLES AND PAMPHLET

The Basis of Value Judgments in Economics. In: **Human Values and Economic Policy: A Symposium**, Sidney Hook, ed. (Proceedings of the 8th Annual New York University Institute of Philosophy, Washington Square, New York, May 1966). New York: New York University Press, 1967, pp. 55-72. CP II, pp. 395-414.

The Boundaries of Social Policy. **Social Work**, 12, 1 (Jan. 1967): 3-11. CP IV, pp. 345-355. RI.

Dare We Take the Social Sciences Seriously? (vice-presidential address, Section K, American Association for the Advancement of Science annual meeting, Washington, D.C., Dec. 1966). **American Behavioral Scientist**, 10, 10 (June 1967): 12-16. CP IV, pp. 357-363. RI.

Divided Views on Tax Increase (letter to the editor). **New York Times**, Oct. 15, 1967, Sec. 4, p. 11.

An Economist Looks at the Future of Sociology. **et al.**, 1, 2 (Winter 1967): 1-6. CP IV, pp. 365-372.

Evolution and Revolution in the Developmental Process. In: **Social Change and Economic Growth** (presentations at the annual meeting of Directors of Development Training and Research Institutes, Bergen, Norway, July 1966). Paris: Development Centre of the Organization for Economic Co-operation and Development, 1967, pp. 19-29. CP V, pp. 217-229.

Human Resources Development as a Learning Process (paper presented at the Human Resources Development Conference, Iowa State University, Oct. 1966). **Farm Policy Forum**, 19, 2 (1966-1967): 27-35. CP III, pp. 339-349. RI.

The Impact of the Draft on the Legitimacy of the National State. In: **The Draft, A Handbook of Facts and Alternatives**, Sol Tax, ed. (Proceedings of the University of Chicago Conference on the Draft, Dec. 1966). Chicago: University of Chicago Press, 1967, pp. 191-196. CP V, pp. 231-236. RI.

Is There a General Theory of Conflict? In: **Industrial Conflict and Race Conflict: Parallels Between the 1930's and the 1960's** (Proceedings of the 1967 Annual Spring Meeting, Detroit, May 1967). Madison, Wisc.: Industrial Relations Research Association, 1967, pp. 4-12.

The Learning and Reality-Testing Process in the International System. **Journal of International Affairs**, 21, 1 (1967): 1-15. BE, pp. 286-302. CP V, pp. 237-253.

The Learning Process in the Dynamics of Total Societies. In: **The Study of Total Societies**, Samuel Z. Klausner, ed. Garden City, N.Y.: Doubleday Anchor Books, 1967, pp. 98-113. CP IV, pp. 373-390.

The Legitimacy of Economics (address presented at the 42nd Western Economic Association annual conference, Boulder, Colo., Aug. 1967). **Western Economic Journal**, 5, 4 (Sept. 1967): 299-307. CP II, pp. 415-425. RI.

Mayer-Boulding Dialogue on Peace Research, Carol Murphy, ed. (Pendle Hill Pamphlet No. 153). Wallingford, Pa.: Pendle Hill, 1967. 30 pp.

The Price System and the Price of the Great Society. In: **The Future of Economic Policy**, Myron H. Ross, ed. (lectures at Western Michigan University, Winter 1966; Michigan Business Papers, No. 44). Ann Arbor: University of Michigan Bureau of Business Research, Graduate School of Business Administration, 1967, pp. 57-73.

The Prospects of Economic Abundance. In: **The Control of Environment: A Discussion at the Nobel Conference**, John D. Roslansky, ed. (held at Gustavus Adolphus College, Jan. 1966). Amsterdam: North-Holland Publishing Company, 1967, pp. 39-57. CP II, pp. 427-445.

The Role of the War Industry in International Conflict. **Journal of Social Issues** (special issue on Conflict and Community in the International System), 23, 1 (Jan. 1967): 47-61. CP V, pp. 255-271. RI.

The Scarcity of Saints. **Gandhi Marg 42,** 11, 2 (Apr. 1967): 162-163.

Technology and the Integrative System. In: **Today's Changing Society, A Challenge to Individual Identity,** Clarence C. Walton, ed. (report of an Arden House conference, Columbia University, Nov. 1966). New York: Institute of Life Insurance, 1967, pp. 57-73. CP IV, pp. 391-409. RI.

The "Two Cultures." In: **Technology in Western Civilization,** Vol. II, Melvin Kranzberg and Carroll W. Pursell, Jr., eds. New York: Oxford University Press, 1967, pp. 686-695. CP IV, pp. 411-422.

The University and Tomorrow's Civilization: Its Role in the Development of a World Community (paper presented at the Higher Education in Tomorrow's World Conference, University of Michigan, Apr. 1967). **Journal of Higher Education,** 38, 9 (Dec. 1967): 477-483. CP V, pp. 281-289. RI.

BOOK REVIEWS

Keeping Book on Social Realities. Review of Raymond A. Bauer, ed., Social Indicators. **Science,** 155, 3762 (Feb. 3, 1967): 550-551.

Milking the Sacred Cow. Review of John Kenneth Galbraith, The New Industrial State. **Book Week,** July 18, 1967, pp. 2, 12.

The Scientific-Military-Industrial Complex. Review of John Kenneth Galbraith, The New Industrial State; and H.L. Nieburg, In the Name of Science. **Virginia Quarterly Review,** 43, 4 (Autumn 1967): 672-679. CP III, pp. 351-360.

Charted Journey Through Theories of Deterrence. Review of Philip Green, Deadly Logic: The Theory of Nuclear Deterrence. **Dissent,** 14, 4 (July-Aug. 1967): 496-498.

Review of Carl G. Gustavson, The Institutional Drive. **Technology and Culture,** 8, 4 (Oct. 1967): 534-535.

Review of Louis J. Halle, The Society of Man. **American Political Science Review,** 61, 3 (Sept. 1967): 843-844.

Fortune Telling. Review of Robert L. Heilbroner, The Limits of American Capitalism. **New York Review of Books,** 7, 12 (Jan. 12, 1967), pp. 29-31.

Neoliberal Economics. Review of John Jewkes, Public and Private Enterprise (Lindsay Memorial Lectures given at the University of Keele, 1964). **Science,** 155, 3766 (Mar. 3, 1967): 1095.

Review of Lester B. Lave, Technological Change: Its Conception and Measurement. **American Journal of Sociology,** 72, 5 (Mar. 1967): 563.

Am I a Man or a Mouse -- Or Both? Review of Konrad Lorenz, On Aggression; and Robert Ardrey, The Territorial Imperative: A Personal Inquiry into the Animal Origins of Property and Nations. **War/Peace Report,** 7, 3 (Mar. 1967): 14-17. CP V, pp. 273-280. RI.

Man Versus Machine. Review of Ben B. Seligman, Most Notorious Victory: Man in an Age of Automation. **New York Times Book Review,** Jan. 1, 1967, p. 25.

Review of G.L.S. Shackle, A Scheme of Economic Theory. **Journal of Business,** 40, 1 (Jan. 1967): 102.

Review of Robert Solo, Economic Organizations and Social Systems. **Science,** 157, 3793 (Sept. 8, 1967): 1158-1159.

VERSE

The Old Agricultural Lag. In: **No Easy Harvest: The Dilemma of Agriculture in Underdeveloped Countries,** by Max Millikan and David Hapgood (based on the Conference on Productivity and Innovation in Agriculture in Underdeveloped Countries, Endicott House, Dedham, Mass., Summer 1964). Boston: Little, Brown and Company, for the Massachusetts Institute of Technology, Center for International Studies, 1967, p. xii.

1968

ARTICLES, MONOGRAPH, AND PAMPHLETS

Accomplishments and Prospects of the Peace Research Movement (with Hanna and Alan Newcombe). **Arms Control and Disarmament,** 1, 1 (1968): 43-58. CP V, pp. 291-308.

America's Economy: The Qualified Uproarious Success. In: **America Now,** John G. Kirk, ed. New York: Atheneum, for Metromedia, 1968, pp. 143-161. CP III, pp. 361-381.

Business and Economic Systems. In: **Positive Feedback,** John H. Milsum, ed. (based on papers presented at a Society for General Systems symposium, American Association for the Advancement of Science annual meeting, Montreal, Dec. 1964). Toronto: Pergamon Press, 1968, pp. 101-117. CP III, pp. 429-447.

The City as an Element in the International System. **Daedalus** (special issue on the Conscience of the City), 97, 4 (Fall 1968): 1111-1123. CP V, pp. 309-323. RI.

Copemanship. **The Center Magazine** (Center for the Study of Democratic Institutions) (July 1968): 60. RI.

Demand and Supply. In: **International Encyclopedia of the Social Sciences,** Vol. 4. New York: Crowell Collier and Macmillan, 1968, pp. 96-104.

The Dynamics of Society. **Bell Telephone Magazine,** 47, 3 (May/June 1968): 4-7. CP IV, pp. 423-428.

The Economics and Financing of Technology in Education: Some Observations. In: **Planning for Effective Utilization of Technology in Education,** Edgar L. Morphet and David L. Jesser, eds. (reports prepared for the National Conference, Denver, May 1961). Denver, Colo.: Designing Education for the Future, 1968, pp. 367-372.

Education for the Spaceship Earth. **Social Education** (special issue on International Education for the Twenty-First Century), 32, 7 (Nov. 1968): 648-652. RI.

The Effects of Military Expenditure Upon the Economic Growth of Japan (edited with Norman Sun; monograph). Tokyo: International Christian University, for the Disarmament Research Team Project, June 1968.

Ethical Dilemmas in Religion and Nationalism (1968 Felix Adler Lecture; pamphlet). New York: Ethical Culture Publications, 1968. 12 pp. RI.

Friends and Social Change (pamphlet). Philadelphia: Friends General Conference of the Religious Society of Friends, 1968. 4 pp.

Grants Versus Exchange in the Support of Education. In: **Federal Programs for the Development of Human Resources**, Vol. 1 (A Compendium of Papers Submitted to the Subcommittee on Economic Progress of the Joint Economic Committee, U.S. Congress). Washington, D.C.: U.S. Government Printing Office, 1968, pp. 232-238. CP III, pp. 383-391.

Greatness as a Pathology of the National Image. In: **U.S. Foreign Policy: Responsibilities of a Superpower in International Politics** (Proceedings of the 1968 World Affairs Conference of North Western Illinois, Dixon-Sterling, Mar. 1968). Champaign: University of Illinois Extension in International Affairs, Sept. 1968, pp. 35-42.

A Historical Note from the President. **American Economic Review**, 58, 5 (Dec. 1968): 1509-1510.

Is Ugliness the Price of Prosperity? In: **Seminar on Environmental Arts and Sciences: Summary of Proceedings** (held in Aspen, Colo., Aug. 1968). Boulder, Colo.: Thorne Ecological Foundation, 1968.

The Legitimation of the Market (C. Woody Thompson Memorial Lecture, Midwest Economics Association annual meeting, Chicago, Apr. 1967). **Nebraska Journal of Economics and Business**, 7, 1 (Spring 1968): 3-14. CP III, pp. 393-406.

Machines, Men and Religion. **Friends Journal**, 14, 24 (Dec. 15, 1968): 643-644.

Man's Choice: Creative Development or Revolution. In: **The United States in a Revolutionary World -- Occasional Papers**, Robert H. Simmons, ed. (papers presented at a California State College conference, Los Angeles, Apr. 1968). Pasadena, Calif.: American Friends Service Committee, 1968, pp. 1-7.

The Many Failures of Success. **Saturday Review**, 51, 47 (Nov. 23, 1968): 29-31. RI.

The "National" Importance of Human Capital. In: **The Brain Drain**, Walter Adams, ed. (papers presented at an international conference, Lausanne, Switz., Aug. 1967). New York: Macmillan, 1968, pp. 109-119. CP II, pp. 461-473. RI.

A Peace Movement in Search of a Party. **War/Peace Report**, 8, 1 (Jan. 1968): 12-13.

Preface to a Special Issue. **Journal of Conflict Resolution** (special review issue), 12, 4 (Dec. 1968): 409-411.

Reflection of the Election -- An Interview with Kenneth Boulding. **Town and Country Review** (Boulder, Colo.), Nov. 14, 1968, pp. 4, 6.

Requirements for a Social Systems Analysis of the Dynamics of the World War Industry. **Peace Research Society (International) Papers** (Cambridge Conference, 1967), Vol. IX (1968): 1-8. RI.

Revolution and Development. In: **Changing Perspectives on Man,** Ben Rothblatt, ed. (1966 Monday Lectures Series). Chicago: University of Chicago Press, 1968, pp. 207-226. CP V, pp. 325-344.

The Role of Economics in the Establishment of Stable Peace. **Economisch-Statistische Berichten** (Rotterdam, Netherlands) (special issue in honor of the 65th birthday of Prof. Dr. J. Tinbergen), 53e, 2639 (Apr. 10, 1968): 332-334. CP III, pp. 407-411.

The Specialist With a Universal Mind (guest editorial; paper presented to the Society for General Systems Research session, American Association for the Advancement of Science annual meeting, New York, Dec. 1967). **Management Science,** 14, 12 (Aug. 1968): B-647 to B-653. RI.

Statement (on Learning, Teaching, Education, and Development). In: **1968 Coloradan,** Vol. 70. Boulder: Associated Students of the University of Colorado, 1968, p. 166.

Town and Country Interviews Dr. Kenneth Boulding. **Town and Country Review** (Boulder, Colo.), Apr. 11, 1968, pp. 1, 11, 13-14; Apr. 18, 1968, pp. 8, 11-12.

The University as an Economic and Social Unit. In: **Colleges & Universities as Agents of Social Change,** W. John Minter and Ian M. Thompson, eds. (papers presented at the 10th Annual College Self-Study Institute, Boulder, Nov. 1968). Boulder, Colo.: Western Interstate Commission for Higher Education, 1968, pp. 75-87; discussion, pp. 89-128. CP III, pp. 413-427.

Values, Technology, and Divine Legitimation. In: **Science, Philosophy, Religion,** Lt. Gerald P. McCarthy, ed. (Proceedings of the 4th Annual Symposium, Sept. 1967). Kirtland Air Force Base, N.M.: Air Force Weapons Laboratory, 1968, pp. 4-16. RI.

What Can We Know and Teach About Social Systems? **Social Science Education Consortium Newsletter** (Boulder, Colo.), 5 (June 1968): 1-5. Also in: **Social Science in the Schools: A Search for Rationale,** Irving Morrissett and W. William Stevens, Jr., eds. (based on papers presented at the Purdue University conference, Feb. 1967). New York: Holt, Rinehart and Winston, 1971, pp. 150-161. CP IV, pp. 429-435. RI.

BOOK

Beyond Economics: Essays on Society, Religion, and Ethics. Ann Arbor: University of Michigan Press, 1968. x + 302 pp. Translation: Japanese. Paperback edition: Ann Arbor Paperbacks, 1970 (nominated for a National Book Award, 1970).

BOOK REVIEWS

Review of Général d'Armée André Beaufre, Deterrence and Strategy, translated from the French by Major-General R.H. Barry; and Arthur H. Dean, Test Ban and Disarmament: The Path of Negotiation. **Political Science Quarterly**, 83, 1 (Mar. 1968): 109-111.

Review of C.E. Black, The Dynamics of Modernization: A Study in Comparative History. **History and Theory**, 7, 1 (1968): 83-90.

Review of David Easton, A Systems Analysis of Political Life. **Behavioral Science**, 13, 2 (Mar. 1968): 147-149.

Observations Unlimited. Review of Eliot Janeway, The Economics of Crisis: War, Politics, and the Dollar. **New York Times Book Review**, 73, 3 (Jan. 21, 1968), p. 24.

"Prognostics": A Guide to Present Action. Review of Herman Kahn and Anthony J. Wiener, The Year 2000: A Framework for Speculation on the Next Thirty-Three Years. **Saturday Review**, 51, 6 (Feb. 10, 1968): 36-37.

In the Money. Review of Ferdinand Lundberg, The Rich and the Super-Rich; and Ben B. Seligman, Permanent Poverty: An American Syndrome. **New York Review of Books**, 11, 4 (Sept. 12, 1968), pp. 40-42.

Asia: Soft States and Hard Facts. Review of Gunnar Myrdal, Asian Drama: An Inquiry into the Poverty Nations. **New Republic**, 158, 18 (May 4, 1968): 25-28. RI.

Review of Report from Iron Mountain on the Possibility and Desirability of Peace. **Trans-action**, 5, 3 (Jan./Feb. 1968): 16. RI.

Review of Gordon Tullock, The Organization of Inquiry. **Journal of Economic Issues**, 2, 2 (June 1968): 259-261.

1969

ARTICLES AND PAMPHLETS

David Fand's "Keynesian Monetary Theories, Stabilization Policy, and the Recent Inflation," A Comment. **Journal of Money, Credit and Banking**, 1, 3 (Aug. 1969): 588-589.

Economic Education: The Stepchild Too is Father of the Man. **Journal of Economic Education**, 1, 1 (Fall 1969): 7-11, CP III, pp. 449-455.

Economics as a Moral Science (presidential address). **American Economic Review** (Papers and Proceedings of the 81st American Economic Association annual meeting, Chicago, Dec. 1968), 59, 1 (Mar. 1969): 1-12. CP II, pp. 447-460. RI.

Education and the Economic Process. In: **The Alternative of Radicalism: Radical and Conservative Possibilities for Teaching the Teachers of**

America's Young Children, Thomas R. Holland and Catherine M. Lee, eds. (Proceedings of the 5th National Conference, Jan. 1969). New Orleans: Tri-University Project in Elementary Education for the U.S. Office of Education, Jan. 1969, pp. 72-82. RI.

Failures and Successes of Economics. **Think,** 35, 3 (May/June 1969): 2-6. RI.

The Fifth Meaning of Love -- Notes on Christian Ethics and Social Policy (paper presented at the Lutheran World Federation Consultation on Christian Ethics and True Humanity, Frankfurt, Germany, Aug. 1968). **Lutheran World,** 16, 3 (July 1969): 219-229. CP IV, pp. 437-449. RI.

The Formation of Values as a Process in Human Learning. In: **Transportation and Community Values** (report of a conference, Airlie House, Warrenton, Va., Mar. 1969). Washington, D.C.: Highway Research Board, National Academy of Sciences, 1969, pp. 31-38; discussion, pp. 39-45. CP III, pp. 457-466.

The Future as Chance and Design (in German; paper presented to the 6th General Assembly and Congress of the International Council of Societies for Industrial Design, London, Sept. 1969). **Bauwelt 50** (Berlin), 60 (Dec. 15, 1969): 1807-1811. CP IV (in English), pp. 525-534.

The Grants Economy (presidential address, Michigan Economics Association, Grand Valley State College, Mar. 1968). **Michigan Academician,** 1, 1 and 2 (Winter 1969): 3-11. CP II, pp. 475-485.

Heretic Among Economists (interview). **Business Week,** 2053 (Jan. 4, 1969): 80-82.

The Interplay of Technology and Values: The Emerging Superculture. In: **Values and the Future: The Impact of Technological Change on American Values,** Kurt Baier and Nicholas Rescher, eds. New York: Free Press, 1969, pp. 336-350. CP IV, pp. 451-467. RI.

An Invitation to Join a New Association for the Study of the Grants Economy. **Association for the Study of the Grants Economy Newsletter,** 1 (Oct. 15, 1969): 2-3.

A Memorandum on the Facilitation of Behavioral Thinking: Four Modest Proposals for Highly Advanced Study (with Richard Christie). **Subterranean Sociology Newsletter** (University of Michigan), 4, 1 (Oct. 1969): 5-8.

Modern Man and Ancient Testimonies. **Quaker Religious Thought,** 11, 1 (Summer 1969): 3-14.

The Need for a University of the Building Industry (presentation to the ACSA Western Region meeting, Boulder, Colo., Nov. 1968). **American Institute of Architects Journal,** 51, 5 (May 1969): 79-81.

Preventing Schismogenesis (comment on Richard Flacks, "Protest or Conform: Some Social Psychological Perspectives on Legitimacy"). **Journal of Applied Behavioral Science,** 5, 2 (Apr./May/June 1969): 151-153. RI.

Public Choice and the Grants Economy: The Intersecting Set. **Public Choice,** 7 (Fall 1969): 1-2. RI.

Research for Peace. **Science Journal** (London), 5A, 4 (Oct. 1969): 53-58. CP V, pp. 345-352.

The Role of Exemplars in the Learning of Community. **World Studies Education Service Bulletin** (London), 10 (Jan. 1969): 15-16.

The Role of Legitimacy in the Dynamics of Society (Graduate School Lecture Series, 1967; pamphlet). University Park: Pennsylvania State University Center for Research, College of Business Administration, 1969. 13 pp. CP IV, pp. 509-523.

The Role of the Church in the Making of Community and Identity (Ethan Allen Cross Memorial Lecture Series; pamphlet). Greeley, Colo.: First Congregational Church, 1969. 8 pp.

Some Unsolved Problems in Economic Education. In: **Five Levels of Incompetence: Report of the 1969 Grove Park Institute,** Thomas Vogt, ed. Washington, D.C.: Consortium of Professional Associations for Study of Special Teacher Improvement Programs (CONPASS), 1971, pp. 37-50.

Stability in International Systems: The Role of Disarmament and Development. In: **International Security Systems: Concepts and Models of World Order,** Richard B. Gray, ed. (based on the Department of Government Lecture Series, Florida State University, 1966-67). Itasca, Ill.: F.E. Peacock, 1969, pp. 193-210. CP V, pp. 353-372.

Statement Before the Subcommittee on Economy in Government of the Joint Economic Committee, U.S. Congress. In: **The Military Budget and National Economic Priorities** (Hearings of the Committee). Washington, D.C.: U.S. Government Printing Office, 1969, Part I, pp. 137-141. CP II, pp. 487-493. RI.

The Task of the Teacher in the Social Sciences. In: **The Quest for Relevance: Effective College Teaching; Vol. III, The Social Sciences.** Washington, D.C.: American Council on Education, for the American Association for Higher Education, Mar. 1969, pp. 3-24. CP IV, pp. 469-490. RI.

Technology and the Changing Social Order. In: **The Urban-Industrial Frontier: Essays on Social Trends and Institutional Goals in Modern Communities,** David Popenoe, ed. (based on the Urban Frontier: 1966-86 Lecture Series, Rutgers University, 1966-67). New Brunswick, N.J.: Rutgers University Press, 1969, pp. 126-140. CP IV, pp. 491-507.

The Threat System. In: **The Cost of Conflict,** John A. Copps, ed. (Department of Economics Lectures, Western Michigan University, Winter Semester 1968; Michigan Business Papers No. 51). Ann Arbor: University of Michigan Bureau of Business Research, 1969, pp. 3-17.

What Don't We Know That Hurts Us? In: **Selected Readings in Economic Education,** Roman F. Warmke and Gerald Draayer, eds. (based on papers presented at the Experienced Teacher Fellowship Program, 1967-68, and a related conference). Athens: Ohio University College of Business Administration, for the Ohio Council on Economic Education, 1969, pp. 3-17.

BOOK REVIEWS

Economics Imperialism. Review of David Braybrooke and Charles E. Lindblom, A Strategy of Decision; Mancur Olson, Jr., The Logic of Collective Action; and

Bruce M. Russett, ed., Economic Theories of International Politics. **Behavioral Science**, 14, 6 (Nov. 1969): 496-500.

A Forecast by Scientists. Review of Nigel Calder, ed., Unless Peace Comes: A Scientific Forecast of New Weapons. **Virginia Quarterly Review**, 45, 1 (Winter 1969): 139-140.

Review of Morton Fried, Marvin Harris and Robert Murphy, eds., War: The Anthropology of Armed Conflict and Aggression. **Comparative Studies in Society and History**, 11, 1 (Jan. 1969): 109-111.

Dialogue with a Marxist. Review of David Horowitz, Empire and Revolution: A Radical Interpretation of Contemporary History. **Book World** (Chicago Tribune), 3, 31 (Aug. 3, 1969): 6.

Tragic Nonsense. Review of Herbert Marcuse, An Essay on Liberation. **New Republic**, 160, 13 (Mar. 29, 1969): 28, 30.

Case Study in Non-Decision. Review of Congressman Richard D. McCarthy, The Ultimate Folly: War by Pestilence, Asphyxiation and Defoliation. **New Republic**, 161, 22 (Nov. 29, 1969): 24-25.

Review of J.E. Meade, The Growing Economy. **Journal of Economic Literature**, 7, 4 (Dec. 1969): 1161-1162.

One of the Great Men. Review of Arthur E. Morgan, Observations. **Religious Humanism**, 3, 2 (Spring 1969): 92.

Growth and Grace: Incompatible? Review of D.B. Robertson, Should Churches Be Taxed?; Alfred Balk, The Religion Business; Nino Lo Bello, The Vatican Empire; and Arthur Herzog, The Church Trap. **Saturday Review**, 52, 6 (Feb. 8, 1969): 27-28.

Review of Kenneth Schneider, Destiny of Change: How Relevant is Man in the Age of Development? **Administrative Science Quarterly**, 14, 2 (June 1969): 318.

Large Projects and Larger Questions. Review of Philip Sporn, Technology, Engineering, and Economics; and Sheldon Novick, The Careless Atom. **Science**, 165, 3892 (Aug. 1, 1969): 483-484.

VERSE

The Ditchley Bank Anthology. **Michigan Business Review**, 21, 2 (Mar. 1969): 17-19. Also: **Journal of Money, Credit and Banking** (conference of university professors of the American Bankers Association, Ditchley Park, Oxfordshire, Eng., Sept. 1968), 1, 3 (Aug. 1968): 354, 462, 507, 555, 624, 681.

X Cantos. **Michigan Quarterly Review**, 8, 1 (Winter 1969): 29-31. RI.

1970

ARTICLES AND PAMPHLET

The Balance of Peace. **Peace Research Society (International) Papers**
(Copenhagen Conference, Aug. 1969), Vol. XIII (1970): 59-65. CP V, pp.
373-381.

Can There Be a National Policy for Stable Peace? **AAUW Journal** (special issue
on Peace), 63, 4 (May 1970): 172-174. CP V, pp. 383-387.

Can We Curb Inflation Without Recession? If So, How? **Denver Post**, Feb. 15,
1970, p. 1.

The Challenge of the Great Transition (in Japanese). **Mainichi Newspapers**
(Tokyo), Mar. 3, 1970, p. 9.

The Crisis of the Universities. **Colorado Quarterly**, 19, 2 (Autumn 1970):
120-129.

The Deadly Industry: War and the International System (introduction). In:
Peace and the War Industry, Kenneth E. Boulding, ed. Chicago: Aldine,
1970, pp. 1-12. RI.

Dialogue (with others). In: **Racism and American Education: A Dialogue and
Agenda for Action**, Kenneth B. Clark, ed. (report of the President's
Commission for the Observance of Human Rights Year Conference, Martha's
Vineyard, Mass., July, 1968). New York: Harper & Row, 1970, pp. 7-145;
Boulding: pp. 30-32, 70, 119-121.

Factors Affecting the Future Demand for Education. In: **Economic Factors
Affecting the Financing of Education**, Vol. 2, Roe L. Johns et al., eds.
Gainesville, Fla.: National Educational Finance Project, 1970, pp. 1-27.
CP III, pp. 503-531. RI.

The Family Segment of the National Economy (address at the American Home
Economics Association annual meeting, Cleveland, June 1970). **Journal of
Home Economics**, 62, 7 (Sept. 1970): 447-454.

Fun and Games with the Gross National Product -- The Role of Misleading
Indicators in Social Policy. In: **The Environmental Crisis: Man's Struggle
to Live with Himself**, Harold W. Helfrich, Jr., ed. (lectures in the 1968-
1969 Symposium in Environmental Crises, Yale University School of
Forestry). New Haven: Yale University Press, 1970, pp. 157-170. CP III,
pp. 467-482.

Fundamental Considerations. In: **Perspectives on Campus Tensions**, David C.
Nichols, ed. Washington, D.C.: American Council on Education, 1970, pp. 3-
17.

Gaps Between Developed and Developing Nations. In: **Toward Century 21:
Technology, Society, and Human Values**, C.S. Wallia, ed. (based on the Human
Values in a Technological Society Lectures, Stanford University, 1968). New
York: Basic Books, 1970, pp. 125-134. CP VI, pp. 11-22.

The Impact of the Defense Industry on the Structure of the American Economy. In: **Adjustments of the U.S. Economy to Reductions in Military Spending,** Bernard Udis, ed. (report prepared for the United States Arms Control and Disarmament Agency, ACDA/E 156), Dec. 1970, pp. 399-433. Also in: **The Economic Consequences of Reduced Military Spending,** Bernard Udis, ed. Lexington, Mass.: D.C. Heath, 1973, pp. 225-252.

Is Economics Culture-Bound? **American Economic Review** (Papers and Proceedings of the 82nd American Economic Association annual meeting, New York, Dec. 1969), 60, 2 (May 1970): 406-411. CP II, pp. 495-502. RI.

The Knowledge Explosion. In: **To Nurture Humaneness: Commitment for the 70's,** Mary-Margaret Scobey and Grace Graham, eds. Washington, D.C.: Association for Supervision and Curriculum Development, National Education Association, 1970, pp. 86-92. CP VI, pp. 39-47.

A Look at National Priorities. **Current History,** 59, 348 (Aug. 1970): 65-72, 111. RI.

A New Ethos for a New Era. In: **Canada and the United States in the World of the Seventies,** R.H. Wagenberg, ed. (Proceedings of the 9th Annual Seminar on Canadian-American Relations, Nov. 1967). Windsor, Ontario: University of Windsor Press, 1970, pp. 91-98. CP VI, pp. 1-10.

No Second Chance for Man. **Progressive** (special issue on the Crisis of Survival), 34, 4 (Apr. 1970): 40-43. RI.

The Philosophy of Peace Research. In: **Proceedings of the International Peace Research Association Third General Conference 1969** (Karlovy Vary, Czech., Sept. 1969), Vol. 1, **Philosophy of Peace Research.** Assen, Netherlands: Van Gorcum, 1970, pp. 5-19. CP V, pp. 389-405. RI.

The Real World of the Seventies and Beyond. In: **Training a Ministry in the Seventies for a World of the Seventies and Beyond: 1969 Conference** (Denver, Oct.-Nov. 1969). New York: Association for Clinical Pastoral Education, 1970, pp. 10-22. CP VI, pp. 23-37.

The Role of the Undergraduate College in Social Change. **Perspectives** (Proceedings of the Association for General and Liberal Studies annual meeting, Colgate University, Oct.-Nov. 1969), 1, 3 (Feb. 1970): 17-20.

The Scientific Revelation (presentation at the Conference on Science and the Morality of Intellect, University of Chicago, Feb. 1970). **Bulletin of the Atomic Scientists,** 26, 7 (Sept. 1970): 13-18. RI.

Social Systems Analysis and the Study of International Conflict. In: **Problems of Modern Strategy** (papers presented at the 10th Annual Conference, St. Catherine's College, Oxford, Sept. 1968; Studies in International Security: 14). London: Chatto and Windus, for The Institute for Strategic Studies, 1970, pp. 77-91. CP VI, pp. 49-65.

Some Functions of the Grants Economy. **Association for the Study of the Grants Economy Newsletter,** 2 (Aug. 15, 1970): 2-4.

Some Hesitant Reflections on the Political Future. In: **1970 Coloradan,** Vol. 72. Boulder: Associated Students of the University of Colorado, 1970, pp. 204-205.

Statement Before the Select Subcommittee on Education of the House Committee on Education and Labor, U.S. Congress. In: **Environmental Quality Education Act of 1970** (Hearings of the Committee). Washington, D.C.: U.S. Government Printing Office, 1970, pp. 597-605. RI.

The War Industry and the American Economy (Third Annual William Carlyle Furnas Memorial Lecture, 1969; pamphlet). De Kalb: Northern Illinois University Department of Economics, 1970. 18 pp. CP III, pp. 483-501.

What Is the GNP Worth? (summary of lecture presented at the University of Pennsylvania, Philadelphia, Apr. 1970). In: **Earth Day -- The Beginning: A Guide for Survival**, National Staff of Environmental Action, eds. New York: Arno Press, Bantam Books, 1970, pp. 143-144.

BOOKS

Economics as a Science. New York: McGraw-Hill, 1970. vii + 161 pp. Edition: Indian. Translations: Chinese, German, Japanese, Korean, Swedish.

Peace and the War Industry (edited, and with an introduction; TRANSaction Book 11). Chicago: Aldine, 1970. ix + 159 pp. See also: Books, 1973.

A Primer on Social Dynamics: History as Dialectics and Development. New York: Free Press, 1970. ix + 153 pp. Translations: Dutch, Japanese.

The Prospering of Truth (Swarthmore Lecture, London Yearly Meeting, Aug. 1970). London: Friends Home Service Committee, 1970. 51 pp.

BOOK REVIEWS

Evolution & Taxes. Review of Peter F. Drucker, The Age of Discontinuity: Guidelines to Our Changing Society; and Herbert Stein, The Fiscal Revolution in America. **TRANSaction**, 7, 6 (Apr. 1970): 81-82.

Review of William R. Ewald, Jr., ed., Environment and Policy: The Next Fifty Years: and Environment and Change: The Next Fifty Years (commissioned on behalf of the American Institute of Planners' Fiftieth Year Consultation). **American Journal of Sociology**, 75, 5 (Mar. 1970): 878-880.

Review of John Hicks, A Theory of Economic History. **American Journal of Agricultural Economics**, 52, 4 (Nov. 1970): 619-620.

Review of Norman Uphoff and Warren F. Ilchman, eds., The Political Economy of Change: Theoretical and Empirical Contributions. **American Political Science Review**, 64, 2 (June 1970): 603-604.

Review of Nathan Leites and Charles Wolf, Jr., Rebellion and Authority: An Analytic Essay on Insurgent Conflicts (a RAND Corporation Research Study). **Annals of the American Academy of Political and Social Science**, 392 (Nov. 1970): 184-185.

Time as a Commodity. Review of Staffan B. Linder, The Harried Leisure Class. **New Republic**, 162, 8 (Feb. 21, 1970): 27-28.

Tantalizing Questions. Review of Margaret Mead, Culture and Commitment: A Study of the Generation Gap. **Virginia Quarterly Review,** 46, 2 (Spring 1970): 339-341.

Tools on a Grand Scale. Review of Emmanuel G. Mesthene, Technological Change: Its Impact on Man and Society (Harvard Studies in Technology and Society). **Science** 168, 3938 (June 19, 1970): 1442.

When Cost Push Comes to Shove. Review of Arthur M. Okun, The Political Economy of Prosperity. **TRANSaction,** 7, 11 (Sept. 1970): 64-68.

1971

ARTICLES AND MONOGRAPH

After Samuelson, Who Needs Adam Smith? (paper presented at the 83rd American Economic Association annual meeting, Detroit, Dec. 1970). **History of Political Economy,** 3, 2 (Fall 1971): 225-237. CP III, pp. 553-567.

The American Economy After Vietnam (presentation at a symposium of the Maxwell Graduate School of Citizenship and Public Affairs, Syracuse University, Feb. 1970). In: **After Vietnam: The Future of American Foreign Policy,** Robert W. Gregg and Charles Kegley, Jr., eds. Garden City, N.Y.: Doubleday Anchor Books, 1971, pp. 307-323.

Discussion (of Allen V. Kneese, "Environmental Pollution: Economics and Policy"). **American Economic Review** (Papers and Proceedings of the 83rd American Economic Association annual meeting, Detroit, Dec. 1970), 61, 2 (May 1971): 167-169.

The Dodo Didn't Make It: Survival and Betterment (presentation at the 3rd Symposium on Science and Society, University of Chicago, Nov. 1970). **Bulletin of the Atomic Scientists,** 27, 5 (May 1971): 19-22.

Environment and Economics. In: **Environment: Resources, Pollution & Society,** William W. Murdoch, ed. Stamford, Conn.: Sinauer Associates, 1971, pp. 359-367. CP III, pp. 569-579.

An Epitaph: The Center for Research on Conflict Resolution, 1959-1971. **Journal of Conflict Resolution,** 15, 3 (Sept. 1971): 279-280.

An Interview with Kenneth E. Boulding. **Seikyo Times** (Tokyo), No. 113 (Jan. 1971): 31-38.

Knowledge as a Road to Peace (keynote address of the COPRED Peace Workshop, Feb. 1971). **Bulletin of the Peace Studies Institute** (Manchester College, Ind.) (Aug. 1971): 1-4.

The Legitimacy of Central Banks. In: **Reappraisal of the Federal Reserve Discount Mechanism,** Vol. 2. Washington, D.C.: Board of Governors of the Federal Reserve System, Dec. 1971, pp. 1-13. CP VI, pp. 67-82.

Letter on "Happiness" (in Japanese). **Sankei Shimbun Newspaper** (Tokyo), Jan. 1, 1971, p. 27.

The Meaning of Human Betterment (Gerald L. Phillippe Memorial Lecture, University of Nebraska-Lincoln, Mar. 1971). **Nebraska Journal of Economics and Business,** 10, 2 (Spring 1971): 3-12. CP IV, pp. 601-612. RI.

The Misallocation of Intellectual Resources in Economics. In: **The Use and Abuse of Social Science,** Irving L. Horowitz, ed. (based on papers presented at a conference on Social Science and National Policy, Rutgers University, Nov. 1969). New York: E.P. Dutton, for TRANSaction Books, 1971, pp. 34-51. CP III, pp. 533-552.

The Need for Reform of National Income Statistics. In: **Proceedings of the Social Statistics Section, 1970** (ASA annual meeting, Detroit, Dec. 1970). Washington, D.C.: American Statistical Association, 1971, pp. 94-97. CP III, pp. 581-586.

People Eyeing 21st Century as Age When Mankind Matures. **Japan Times** (Tokyo), Jan. 1, 1971, p. 6.

The Pursuit of Happiness and the Value of the Human Being (in Japanese). **Nihon Keizei Shimbun** (Japan Economic Journal; Tokyo), Jan. 1, 1971, Supplement 2, p. 39.

Toward a Modest Society: The End of Growth and Grandeur. In: **Economic Perspectives of Boulding and Samuelson** (Davidson Lectures -- 1970-71). Durham: Whittemore School of Business and Economics, University of New Hampshire, 1971, pp. 7-20; reply, pp. 21-22. CP VI, pp. 83-98.

Toward the Year 2000 (presentation at the National Council for the Social Studies annual meeting, Houston, Nov. 1969; SSEC Monograph Series, Publication No. 132). Boulder, Colo.: Social Science Education Consortium, 1971. 14 pp.

Unprofitable Empire, Britain in India 1880-1967: A Critique of the Hobson-Lenin Thesis on Imperialism (with Tapan Mukerjee). **Peace Research Society (International) Papers** (Rome Conference, 1970), Vol. XVI (1971): 1-21.

What Do Economic Indicators Indicate?: Quality and Quantity in the GNP. In: **The Economics of Pollution** (1971 Charles C. Moskowitz Lectures). New York: New York University Press, 1971, pp. 31-80.

Where Does Development Lead? **Les Carnets de l'enfance** (Assignment Children; Paris, UNICEF), 13 (Jan.-Mar. 1971): 48-57; summaries in French, Spanish and German, pp. 58-62.

A World-Famous "Economist-Philosopher" Gives His Views on Religion, Radicalism, the Hippies and More (interview). **Seikyo Times** (Tokyo), 113 (Jan. 1971): 31-32, 37-38.

BOOKS

Kenneth E. Boulding Collected Papers, Vol. I: Economics (1932-1955), Fred R. Glahe, ed. Boulder: Colorado Associated University Press, 1971. xi + 492 pp.

Kenneth E. Boulding Collected Papers, Vol. II: Economics (1956-1970), Fred R. Glahe, ed. Boulder: Colorado Associated University Press, 1971. viii + 510 pp.

BOOK REVIEWS

Living With Violence. Review of Hannah Arendt, On Violence; and E.V. Walter, Terror and Resistance: A Study of Political Violence. **War/Peace Report**, 11, 6 (June/July 1971): 17-18.

Review of Gottfried Dietze, Youth, University, and Democracy; Algo D. Henderson, The Innovative Spirit; and Lewis B. Mayhew, Arrogance on Campus. **American Association of University Professors Bulletin**, 57, 2 (June 1971): 296-297.

Review of E.J. Hobsbawm, Industry and Empire: An Economic History of Britain Since 1750. **History and Theory**, 10, 1 (1971): 147-149.

Review of John R. Platt, Perception and Change: Projections for Survival. **Michigan Quarterly Review**, 10, 4 (Fall 1971): 295-297.

Economists at a Family Picnic. Review of Joan Robinson, Economic Heresies: Some Old-Fashioned Questions in Economic Theory. **Business Week**, 2177 (May 22, 1971): 12.

The Intellectual Framework of Bad Political Advice. Review of W.W. Rostow, Politics and the Stages of Growth. **Virginia Quarterly Review**, 47, 4 (Autumn 1971): 602-607.

1972

ARTICLES AND PAMPHLET

Economics and General Systems. In: **The Relevance of General Systems Theory: Papers Presented to Ludwig von Bertalanffy on His Seventieth Birthday**, Ervin Laszlo, ed. New York: George Braziller, 1972, pp. 77-92. RI.

Economics as a Not Very Biological Science. In: **Challenging Biological Problems: Directions Toward Their Solution**, John A. Behnke, ed. (25th Anniversary volume). New York: Oxford University Press, for the American Institute of Biological Sciences, 1972, pp. 357-375.

Future Directions (with Martin Pfaff). In: **Redistribution to the Rich and the Poor: The Grants Economics of Income Distribution**, Kenneth Boulding and Martin Pfaff, eds. (Grants Economics Series). Belmont, Calif.: Wadsworth, 1972, pp. 387-390.

The Future of Personal Responsibility. **American Behavioral Scientist** (special issue on Changing Attitudes Toward Personal Responsibility; presentations at the Insurance Company of North America Conference, Philadelphia, May 1971), 15, 3 (Jan./Feb. 1972): 329-359. CP IV, pp. 535-567.

Grants Economics: A Simple Introduction (with Martin Pfaff and Janos Horvath). **American Economist**, 16, 1 (Spring 1972): 19-28. RI.

The Grants Economy and the Development Gap (with Martin Pfaff). In: **The Gap Between Rich and Poor Nations**, Gustav Ranis, ed. (Proceedings of the International Economic Association Conference, Bled, Yugoslavia, 1970). London: Macmillan Press, 1972, pp. 143-170.

The Household as Achilles' Heel (premier lecture of the Colston E. Warne lecture series, American Council on Consumer Interests annual conference, Dallas, Apr. 1972). **Journal of Consumer Affairs**, 6, 2 (Winter 1972): 110-119. CP VI, pp. 117-128.

How Things Go From Bad to Worse. In: **Recycle This Book!: Ecology, Society, and Man**, J. David Allan and Arthur J. Hanson, eds. (based on presentations at the ENACT Environmental Teach-In, Ann Arbor, Mich., Mar. 1970). Belmont, Calif.: Wadsworth Publishing Company, 1972, pp. 131-133.

Human Betterment and the Quality of Life. In: **Human Behavior in Economic Affairs: Essays in Honor of George Katona**, Burkhard Strumpel, James N. Morgan and Ernest Zahn, eds. Amsterdam: Elsevier Scientific, 1972, pp. 455-470. CP VI, pp. 99-116.

Introduction. In: **Economic Imperialism: A Book of Readings**, Kenneth Boulding and Tapan Mukerjee, eds. Ann Arbor: University of Michigan Press, 1972, pp. ix-xviii.

Introduction. In: **Analysis of the Problem of War**, by Clyde Eagleton (Garland Edition). New York: Garland, 1972, pp. 5-7.

Japan Should Produce "Things" With Value Rather Than a "Strong Yen" (interview in Japanese). **Nikkei Business** (Tokyo), Dec. 25, 1972, pp. 63-65.

Kenneth Boulding: The Arrival of Spaceship Earth (interview). In: **Philosophers of the Earth: Conversations with Ecologists**, by Anne Chisholm. New York: E.P. Dutton, 1972, pp. 25-38.

The Liberal Arts Amid a Culture in Crisis. **Liberal Education** (Proceedings of the 58th Association of American Colleges annual meeting, Washington, D.C., Jan. 1972), 58, 1 (Mar. 1972): 5-17. CP VI, pp. 129-143.

Man as a Commodity. In: **Human Resources and Economic Welfare: Essays in Honor of Eli Ginzberg**, Ivar Berg, ed. New York: Columbia University Press, 1972, pp. 35-49. CP III, pp. 587-603.

The "Mantle of Elijah" Complex. In: **Recycle This Book!: Ecology, Society, and Man**, J. David Allan and Arthur J. Hanson, eds. (based on presentations at the ENACT Environmental Teach-In, Ann Arbor, Mich., Mar. 1970). Belmont, Calif.: Wadsworth Publishing Company, 1972, pp. 162-163.

New Goals for Society? In: **Energy, Economic Growth, and the Environment**, Sam H. Schurr, ed. (papers presented at an RFF Forum, Washington, D.C., Apr. 1972). Baltimore: Johns Hopkins University Press, for Resources for the Future, 1972, pp. 139-151. CP IV, pp. 585-599. RI.

The Role of the Social Sciences in the Control of Technology (paper presented at the American Association for the Advancement of Science annual meeting, Boston, Dec. 1969). In: **Technology and Man's Future**, Albert H. Teich, ed. New York: St. Martin's Press, 1972, pp. 263-274. CP VI, pp. 187-200.

The Schooling Industry as a Possibly Pathological Section of the American Economy (paper presented at the American Educational Research Association annual meeting, New York, Feb. 1971). **Review of Educational Research**, 42, 1 (Apr. 1972): 129-143. CP IV, pp. 569-584.

The Three Faces of Power. In: **50 Years of War Resistance: What Now?** London: War Resisters' International, 1972, pp. 18-21.

Toward a Theory for the Study of Community. In: **Issues in Community Organization**, Lawrence Witmer, ed. (papers prepared for the University of Chicago Conference on Community Organization, Spring 1968). Chicago: Center for the Scientific Study of Religion, 1972, pp. 23-31.

Toward the Development of a Cultural Economics. **Social Science Quarterly** (special issue including a symposium on the Idea of Culture in the Social Sciences), 53, 2 (Sept. 1972): 267-284. CP VI, pp. 145-164. RI.

Towards a Pure Theory of Foundations (paper prepared for the Kettering Foundation Conference on Foundations, Dayton, Nov. 1970; pamphlet). Danbury, Conn.: Non-Profit Report, 1972, 22 pp. (included with **Non-Profit REPORT**, 5, 3, Mar. 1972). CP VI, pp. 165-186. RI.

Towards a Twenty-First Century Politics (40th Lecture on Research and Creative Work, University of Colorado, Apr. 1971). **Colorado Quarterly**, 20, 3 (Winter 1972): 309-319. CP V, pp. 407-419. RI.

The Weapon as an Element in the Social System (presentation at the colloquium on Multipolar Strategy, Institute of International Studies, University of California, Berkeley, Mar. 1970). In: **The Future of the International Strategic System**, Richard Rosecrance, ed. San Francisco: Chandler, 1972, pp. 81-92.

BOOKS

The Appraisal of Change (lectures given for the Japan Broadcast Company, Oct. 1970; in Japanese). Tokyo: Nippon Hoso Shuppan Kyokai (Japan Broadcast Publishing Company), 1972. 176 pp.

Economic Imperialism: A Book of Readings (edited with Tapan Mukerjee). Ann Arbor: University of Michigan Press, 1972. xviii + 338 pp.

Redistribution to the Rich and the Poor: The Grants Economics of Income Distribution (edited with Martin Pfaff; Grants Economics Series). Belmont, Calif.: Wadsworth, 1972. 390 pp. Translation: Japanese.

BOOK REVIEWS

Review of Martin Bronfenbrenner, Income Distribution Theory. **Journal of Economic Issues**, 6, 2 and 3 (Sept. 1972): 123-128.

The Wolf of Rome. Review of Jay W. Forrester, World Dynamics. **Business and Society Review**, 2 (Summer 1972): 106-109.

Search for Time's Arrow. Review of Nicholas Georgescu-Roegen, The Entropy Law and the Economic Process. **Science**, 175, 4026 (Mar. 10, 1972): 1099-1100.

The Gospel of St. Malthus. Review of Garrett Hardin, Exploring New Ethics for Survival: The Voyage of the Spaceship Beagle. **New Republic**, 167, 9 (Sept. 9, 1972): 22-25.

A Devil Theory of Economic History. Review of Michael Hudson, Super Imperialism: The Economic Strategy of American Empire. **Book World** (Washington Post), 7, 53 (Dec. 31, 1972): 7, 13.

Review of Fred Charles Iklé, Every War Must End. **Political Science Quarterly**, 87, 4 (Dec. 1972): 705-707.

Yes, The Wolf is Real. Review of Donella and Dennis Meadows, Jørgen Randers, and William W. Behrens III, The Limits to Growth. **New Republic**, 166, 18 (Apr. 29, 1972): 27-28.

Review of Bruce Russett, What Price Vigilance? The Burdens of National Defense. **American Political Science Review**, 66, 1 (Mar. 1972): 217.

VERSE

A Ballad of Ecological Awareness. In: **The Careless Technology: Ecology and International Development**, M. Taghi Farvar and John P. Milton, eds. (record of the Conference on the Ecological Aspects of International Development, Airlie House, Warrenton, Va., Dec. 1968). Garden City, N.Y.: Natural History Press, for the Conservation Foundation and the Center for the Biology of Natural Systems, Washington University, 1972, pp. 3, 157, 371, 669, 793, 955.

New Goals for Society? In: **Energy, Economic Growth, and the Environment**, Sam H. Schurr, ed. (papers presented at an RFF forum, Washington, D.C., Apr. 1971). Baltimore: Johns Hopkins University Press, for Resources for the Future, 1972, p. 139. CP IV, p. 587. RI.

1973

ARTICLES AND MONOGRAPH

Aristocrats Have Always Been Sons of Bitches (interview with Robert W. Glasgow). **Psychology Today**, 6, 8 (Jan. 1973): 60-64, 67-68, 70, 86-87. RI.

ASGE -- In Retrospect and Prospect. **Association for the Study of the Grants Economy Newsletter**, 5 (Dec. 5, 1973): 2-3.

Can There Be a Growth Policy? In: **Man and His Environment: The Vail Experience** (summary of the 3rd Vail Symposium, Aug. 1973). Vail, Colo.: The Printery, for the Town of Vail, 1973, p. 19.

The Challenge of Change (Lecture 10 in "America and the Future of Man" Course By Newspaper). Distributed by Copley News Service for the Regents of the University of California in all major newspapers in the U.S., Dec. 6, 1973. RI.

Communication of the Integrative Network. In: **Communication: Ethical and Moral Issues**, Lee Thayer, ed. (based on a colloquia series at the Center for Advanced Study of Communication, University of Iowa, Iowa City, 1969-70). New York: Gordon and Breach, 1973, pp. 201-213. CP VI, pp. 201-217.

Economic Theory of Natural Liberty. In: **Dictionary of the History of Ideas**, Vol. II, Philip P. Wiener, ed.-in-chief. New York: Charles Scribner's Sons, 1973, pp. 61-71. CP VI, pp. 249-273.

The Economics of Ecology. In: **Final Conference Report for the National Conference on Managing the Environment** (Washington, D.C., May 1973). Washington, D.C.: Office of Research and Development, U.S. Environmental Protection Agency, 1973, pp. 11-13 to 11-17. RI.

The Economics of Energy. **Annals of the American Academy of Political and Social Science** (special issue on the Energy Crisis: Reality or Myth), 410 (Nov. 1973): 120-126.

Equality and Conflict. **Annals of the American Academy of Political and Social Science** (special issue on Income Inequality), 409 (Sept. 1973): 1-8. CP VI, pp. 219-227.

Foreword. In: **Image and Environment: Cognitive Mapping and Spatial Behavior**, Roger M. Downs and David Stea, eds. Chicago: Aldine, 1973, pp. vii-ix.

Foreword. In: **The People: Growth and Survival**, by Gerhard Hirschfeld. Chicago: Aldine, for the Council for the Study of Mankind, 1973, pp. xiii-xvi.

Foreword. In: **The Image of the Future**, by Fred Polak, translated from the Dutch and abridged by Elise Boulding. San Francisco and Amsterdam: Jossey Bass/Elsevier, 1973, pp. v-vi.

General Systems as an Integrating Force in the Social Sciences. In: **University Through Diversity: A Festschrift for Ludwig von Bertalanffy**, Vol. II, William Gray and Nicholas D. Rizzo, eds. New York: Gordon & Breach, 1973. pp. 951-967. CP VI, pp. 229-247.

Intersects: The Peculiar Organizations. In: **Challenge to Leadership: Managing in a Changing World** (A Conference Board Study). New York: Free Press, for the Conference Board, 1973, pp. 179-201. RI.

Interview: Kenneth E. Boulding. In: **Economics 73-74: Text**. Guilford, Conn.: Dushkin, 1973, pp. 10-11.

Introduction. In: **Poverty and Progress: An Ecological Perspective on Economic Development**, by Richard G. Wilkinson. New York: Praeger, 1973, pp. xiii-xx.

Love, Fear and the Economist (interview). **Challenge**, 16, 3 (July-Aug. 1973): 32-39.

Organization Theory as a Bridge Between Socialist and Capitalist Societies. **Journal of Management Studies**, 10, 1 (Feb. 1973): 1-7.

Role Prejudice as an Economic Problem (Part I of "Combatting Role Prejudice and Sex Discrimination: Findings of the American Economic Association

Committee on the Status of Women in the Economics Profession). **American Economic Review,** 63, 5 (Dec. 1973): 1049-1053.

The Shadow of the Stationary State. **Daedalus** (special issue on The No-Growth Society), 102, 4 (Fall 1973): 89-101. RI.

Social Dynamics. In: **Summer School in Peace Research: Grindstone Island 1973** (report on the 4th Annual Summer School, June-July 1973). Dundas, Ont.: Canadian Peace Research Institute, Nov. 1973, p. 26.

Social Risk, Political Uncertainty, and the Legitimacy of Private Profit (paper presented at the Public Utility Conference, East Lansing, Feb. 1971). In: **Risk and Regulated Firms,** R. Hayden Howard, ed. East Lansing: Michigan State University Graduate School of Business Administration, 1973, pp. 82-93. CP VI, pp. 275-288.

System Analysis and Its Use in the Classroom (with Alfred Kuhn and Lawrence Senesh; SSEC Monograph Series, Publication No. 157). Boulder, Colo.: Social Science Education Consortium, 1973. 58 pp. RI.

A Theory of Prediction Applied to the Future of Economic Growth. In: **International Symposium "New Problems of Advanced Societies"** (Tokyo, Nov. 1972). Tokyo: Japan Economic Research Institute, 1973, pp. 53-61. CP VI, pp. 289-299.

BOOKS

Kenneth E. Boulding Collected Papers, Vol. III: Political Economy, Larry D. Singell, ed. Boulder: Colorado Associated University Press, 1973. ix + 614 pp.

The Economy of Love and Fear: A Preface to Grants Economics (Grants Economics Series). Belmont, Calif.: Wadsworth Publishing Company, 1973. 116 pp. Translations: Japanese, Spanish.

Peace and the War Industry. 2nd edition (edited, and with a revised introduction; Transaction/Society Book Series -- 11). New Brunswick, N.J.: Transaction Books, 1973. 213 pp. See also: Books, 1970.

Transfers in an Urbanized Economy (edited with Martin and Anita Pfaff; Grants Economics Series). Belmont, Calif.: Wadsworth Publishing Company, 1973. 376 pp. Translation: Japanese.

BOOK REVIEWS

Multiply and Replenish: Alternative Perspectives on Population. Review of Howard M. Bahr, Bruce A. Chadwick, and Darwin L. Thomas, eds., Population Resources and the Future Non-Malthusian Perspectives. **Dialogue: A Journal of Mormon Thought,** 8, 3/4 (1973): 159-163.

Global Economics: A Failure So Far. Review of Jagdish N. Bhagwati, ed., Economics and World Order: From the 1970's to the 1990's. **War/Peace Report,** 12, 5 (July/Aug. 1973): 30-31.

Review of William Breit and Roger L. Ransom, The Academic Scribblers: American Economists in Collision. **Journal of Political Economy**, 81, 4 (July/Aug. 1973): 1041-1042.

Review of Lester R. Brown, World Without Borders. **International Development Review**, 15, 2 (1973): 30.

Zoom, Gloom, Doom and Room. Review of H.S.D. Cole, Christopher Freeman, Marie Jahoda, and K.L.R. Pavitt, eds., Models of Doom: A Critique of the Limits to Growth; Ralph E. Lapp, The Logarithmic Century: Charting Future Shock; and John Maddox, The Doomsday Syndrome. **New Republic**, 169, 6 (Aug. 11, 1973): 25-27.

Review of Edgar S. Dunn, Jr., Economic and Social Development: A Process of Social Learning. **Urban Studies** (Glasgow), 10, 1 (Feb. 1973): 105-106.

Big Families Do Pay. Review of Bernard James, The Death of Progress; Mahmood Mamdani, The Myth of Population Control: Family, Caste, and Class in an Indian Village; and Herbert N. Woodward, The Human Dilemma. **New Republic**, 168, 9 (Mar. 3, 1973): 22-23.

Review of Richard A. Peterson, The Industrial Order and Social Policy. **Administrative Science Quarterly**, 18, 4 (Dec. 1973): 555-556.

Review of John Rawls, A Theory of Justice. **Journal of Economic Issues**, 7, 4 (Dec. 1973): 667-673.

Review of G.L.S. Shackle, Epistemics & Economics: A Critique of Economic Doctrines. **Journal of Economic Literature**, 11, 4 (Dec. 1973): 1373-1374.

VERSE

COPRED, A Prophecy (written at the Consortium on Peace Research, Education and Development Advisory Council meeting, Windsor, Ontario, Apr. 1973). **Peace and Change**, 1, 2 (Spring 1973): 60.

Reflections. In: **Final Conference Report for the National Conference on Managing the Environment** (Washington, D.C., May 1973). Washington, D.C.: Office of Research and Development, U.S. Environmental Protection Agency, 1973, p. iii.

1974

ARTICLES AND MONOGRAPH

Bottleneck Economics. **Technology Review**, 76, 6 (May 1974): 16-17.

Defense Against Unwanted Change (Karl Taylor Compton Lecture, Feb. 1974). Cambridge, Mass.: Technology and Culture Seminar, Massachusetts Institute of Technology, 1974. 16 pp.

The Doubtful Future (Addison L. Roache Lecture, Indiana University-Purdue University, Indianapolis, Mar. 1974). **Review** (Alumni Association of the

College of Arts and Sciences, Graduate School, Indiana University Bloomington, Ind.), 16, 4 (Summer 1974): 27-37.

ECON is a Four-Letter Word. In: **Increasing Understanding of Public Problems and Policies -- 1973** (based on presentations at the 23rd National Public Policy Conference, planned by the National Public Policy Education Committee, Gull Lake, Brainerd, Minn., Sept. 1973). Chicago: Farm Foundation, 1974, pp. 137-146.

Ethics of Growth. **Technology Review,** 76, 4 (Feb. 1974): 10, 83.

Foreword. In: **Creative Tension: The Life and Thought of Kenneth Boulding,** by Cynthia Kerman. Ann Arbor: University of Michigan Press, 1974, pp. v-vii.

Foreword. In: **The Logic of Social Systems,** by Alfred Kuhn. San Francisco: Jossey-Bass, 1974, pp. ix-xi.

Future Education Pattern at Metropolitan State College (letter to the editor). **Denver Post,** Sept. 14, 1974, p. 8.

Imagining Failure, Successfully. **Technology Review,** 76, 7 (June 1974): 8.

Interview: Kenneth E. Boulding. In: **The Study of Society.** Guilford, Conn.: Dushkin Publishing Group, 1974, pp. 491-493. RI.

Introducing Freshmen to the Social System (with Elise Boulding). **American Economic Review** (Papers and Proceedings of the 86th American Economic Association annual meeting, New York, Dec. 1973), 64, 2 (May 1974): 414-419.

Introduction (to A Trans-Atlantic Dialogue: International Relations and the World Society; videotape based on the roundtable discussion conducted at the International Studies Association annual meeting, St. Louis, Mar. 1974). St. Louis: Center for International Studies, University of Missouri-St. Louis, 1974.

Introduction to the Global Society: Interdisciplinary Perspectives (with Elise Boulding; monograph; Learning Package Series Number 1). St. Louis: Consortium for International Education, Center for International Studies, University of Missouri-St. Louis, 1974. 42 pp.

Kenneth E. Boulding (interview). In: **On Growth: The Crisis of Exploding Population and Resource Depletion,** Willem L. Oltmans, ed. New York: G.P. Putnam's Sons/Capricorn Books, 1974, pp. 437-441.

Land as a Servant of Man: A Systematic Look at Land Use. In: **Land Use in Colorado: The Planning Thicket,** Thomas R. Kitsos, ed. (Proceedings of the 16th Annual Institute of Planning Officials, Estes Park, Colo., Oct. 1973). Boulder: Bureau of Governmental Research, University of Colorado, 1974, pp. 11-17.

The Learning of Peace (presidential address delivered at the International Studies Association annual meeting, St. Louis, Mar. 1974). **International Studies Notes,** 1, 2 (Summer 1974): 1-8. CP VI, pp. 301-318.

Plains of Science, Summits of Passion. **Technology Review,** 77, 2 (Dec. 1974): 6. RI.

Pricing in the Energy Crisis. **Technology Review**, 76, 5 (Mar./Apr. 1974): 8.

A Program for Justice Research (paper presented at the International Peace Research Association Fifth General Conference, Varanasi, India, Jan. 1974). **Bulletin of Peace Proposals**, 5 (1974): 64-72. CP VI, pp. 329-339.

The Quality of Life and Economic Affluence. In: **Environmental Spectrum: Social and Economic Views on the Quality of Life**, Ronald O. Clarke and Peter List, eds. (papers presented at the Symposium on Economic Growth and the Quality of Life, Oregon State University, Corvallis, May 1973). New York: D. Van Nostrand, 1974, pp. 82-95. CP VI, pp. 341-356.

Reflections on Planning: The Value of Uncertainty. **Technology Review**, 77, 1 (Oct./Nov. 1974): 8. RI.

The Social System and the Energy Crisis. **Science** (special issue on Energy), 184, 4134 (Apr. 19, 1974): 255-257. RI.

The Theory of Human Betterment. **Technology Review**, 76, 8 (July/Aug. 1974): 8, 63.

Universities, University Knowledge, and the Human Future. **Lux Mundi** (Seoul, Korea), 3, 2 (Feb. 1974): 9-12.

What Went Wrong, If Anything, Since Copernicus? (paper presented at the AAAS Symposium on Science, Development and Human Values, Mexico City, July 1973). **Bulletin of the Atomic Scientists**, 30, 1 (Jan. 1974): 17-23. Also available on tape in the "Speaking of Science: Conversations With Outstanding Scientists" series, Vol. III. Washington, D.C.: American Association for the Advancement of Science, 1973. CP VI, pp. 319-327.

The World as an Economic Region. In: **Regional Economic Policy: Proceedings of a Conference** (Minneapolis, Nov. 1973). Minneapolis: Federal Reserve Bank of Minneapolis, June 1974, pp. 27-34.

BOOK

Kenneth E. Boulding Collected Papers, Vol. IV: Toward a General Social Science, Larry D. Singell, ed. Boulder: Colorado Associated University Press, 1974. vii + 623 pp.

BOOK REVIEWS

Review of Daniel Bell, The Coming of Post-Industrial Society, A Venture in Social Forecasting. **Journal of Economic Issues**, 8, 4 (Dec. 1974): 952-953.

Defense Spending: Burden or Boon? Review of Emile Benoit, Defense and Economic Growth in Developing Countries. **War/Peace Report**, 13, 1 (June 1974): 19-21.

Review of Bernard Brodie, War & Politics. **Friends Journal**, 20, 3 (Feb. 1, 1974): 77-78.

Review of Wilson Clark, Energy for Survival: The Alternative to Extinction. **Smithsonian**, 5, 7 (Oct. 1974): 130.

Review of Alexander Eckstein, ed., Comparison of Economic Systems: Theoretical and Methodological Approaches. **Political Science Quarterly,** 89, 1 (Mar. 1974): 236-238.

Minus the Spark. Review of John Kenneth Galbraith, Economics & the Public Purpose. **Monthly Labor Review,** 97, 10 (Oct. 1974): 80-81.

Review of Gene Sharp, The Politics of Non-Violent Action; and R.S. Sampson, The Discovery of Peace. **Armed Forces and Society,** 1, 1 (Fall 1974): 139-144.

Review of Ben Whitaker, The Philanthropoids: Foundations and Society. **Chronicle of Higher Education,** 9, 2 (Sept. 30, 1974): 10.

1975

ARTICLES

Can Peace Be Taught? **Thresholds,** 1, 2 (Apr./May 1975): 8-9.

The Clouded Future of the American Economy: Implications for Older Consumers. In: **Proceedings of the National Forum on Consumer Concerns of Older Americans, Washington, D.C., June 1-3, 1975.** Washington, D.C.: National Retired Teachers Association/American Association of Retired Persons, 1975, pp. 13-31; discussion, pp. 31-35.

Comment (on Gunnar Myrdal, "The Unity of the Social Sciences"). **Human Organization,** 34, 4 (Winter 1975): 332.

A Curmudgeon Stick (comment). **Challenge,** 18, 4 (Sept./Oct. 1975): 55.

Dialogue -- Civilized Society (with John Kenneth Galbraith). **Mainichi Daily News** (English edition) and **Mainichi Shimbun** (Japanese edition). Serialized beginning October 14, 1975; ending December 27, 1975 (61 segments).

Doers and Stoppers. **Technology Review,** 78, 1 (Oct./Nov. 1975): 8.

Economics and the Ecosystem (guest editorial). In: **Living in the Environment: Concepts, Problems, and Alternatives,** by G. Tyler Miller, Jr. Belmont, Calif.: Wadsworth Publishing Company, 1975, pp. 327-328. RI.

Entropy Economics. In: **Public Utility Regulation: Change and Scope,** Werner Sichel and Thomas G. Gies, eds. (papers presented at a seminar, Western Michigan University, May 1974). Lexington, Mass.: Lexington Books/D.C. Heath, 1975, pp. 1-12.

Envisioning the Future (interview). **Cultural Information Service** (newsletter) (Mar. 1975): 6-8.

The Evaluation of Large Systems. **Technology Review,** 77, 6 (May 1975): 12, 69.

The High Price of Technology Misused. **Technology Review,** 77, 8 (July/Aug. 1975): 5.

The International System in the Eighties: Models of International Peace. In: **Dynamics of a Conflict,** Gabriel Sheffer, ed. Atlantic Highlands, N.J.: Humanities Press, 1975, pp. 3-18. CP VI, pp. 357-374.

Introduction: Thirsting for the Testable. In: **Comparative Public Policy: Issues, Theories, and Methods,** Craig Liske, William Loehr and John McCamant, eds. New York: John Wiley/Halsted Press, for Sage Publications, 1975, pp. 7-10.

Introduction. In: **Adjustments of Colorado School Districts to Declining Enrollments,** by Mark Rodekohr (monograph). Lincoln: Nebraska Curriculum Development Center, University of Nebraska, for the Academic Disciplines Committee of the Study Commission on Undergraduate Education and the Education of Teachers, 1975, pp. 1-8.

Justification for Inequality: The Contributions of Economic Theory (lecture at MIT, Dec. 1974). Cambridge, Mass.: Technology and Culture Seminar, Massachusetts Institute of Technology, 1975. 16 pp.

The Management of Decline (based on an address to the Regents Convocation of the University of the State of New York, Albany, Sept. 1974). **Change,** 7, 5 (June 1975): 8-9, 64. RI.

Notes on the Present State of Neoclassical Economics as a Subset of the Orthodox. **Journal of Economic Issues,** 9, 2 (June 1975): 223-228. RI.

Predictive Reliability and the Future: The Need for Uncertainty. In: **The Future of Education: Perspectives on Tomorrow's Schooling,** Louis Rubin, ed. (based on papers presented at the Alternative Futures of Education: Symposium '73, Philadelphia, Oct. 1973). Boston: Allyn and Bacon, for Research for Better Schools, 1975, pp. 54-74; editorial commentary, pp. 75-81.

The Pursuit of Equality. In: **The Personal Distribution of Income and Wealth,** James D. Smith, ed. (NBER Conference, Pennsylvania State University, Oct. 1972; Studies in Income and Wealth, Vol. 39). New York: National Bureau of Economic Research, 1975, pp. 11-28. CP VI, pp. 375-394.

Quality Versus Equality: The Dilemma of the University. **Daedalus** (special issue on American Higher Education: Toward an Uncertain Future, Vol. II), 104, 1 (Winter 1975): 298-303.

The Report of the President (presentation at the International Studies Association annual business meeting, Washington, D.C., Feb. 1975). **International Studies Newsletter,** 2, 1 (Mar. 1975): 1.

Some Observations on the Learning of Economics. **American Economic Review** (Papers and Proceedings of the 87th American Economic Association annual meeting, San Francisco, Dec. 1974), 65, 2 (May 1975): 428-430.

A Spectrum of Strategies for Research Grants. **Technology Review,** 77, 4 (Feb. 1975): 12.

The Stability of Inequality (paper presented at the Association for Social Economics session, Allied Social Sciences Association annual meeting, San Francisco, Dec. 28, 1974). **Review of Social Economy,** 33, 1 (Apr. 1975): 1-14. RI.

A Technology for Educational Art? **Technology Review**, 77, 7 (June 1975): 5.

Toward a Theory of Research Grants? **Technology Review**, 77, 3 (Jan. 1975): 5.

Trim "War Industry," Help the Economy. **Los Angeles Times**, Jan. 5, 1975, Part VIII, p. 5. RI.

Truth or Power? (editorial). **Science**, 190, 4213 (Oct. 31, 1975): 423.

What Are Resources? **Forensic Quarterly**, 49, 3 (Aug. 1975): 263-268.

What Do We Know When We Know a Number? **Technology Review**, 78, 2 (Dec. 1975): 10. RI.

BOOKS

Kenneth E. Boulding Collected Papers, Vol. V: International Systems: Peace, Conflict Resolution, and Politics, Larry D. Singell, ed. Boulder: Colorado Associated University Press, 1975. x + 497 pp.

Sonnets from the Interior Life and Other Autobiographical Verse. See: Verse.

BOOK REVIEWS

What's the Result? Review of Frank S. Levy, Arnold J. Meltsner, and Aaron Wildavsky, Urban Outcomes: Schools, Streets and Libraries (The Oakland Project). **Working Papers for a New Society**, 3, 2 (Summer 1975): 64-65.

Conditional Optimism About the World Situation. Review of Mihajlo Mesarovic and Eduard Pestel, Mankind at the Turning Point (Second Report to the Club of Rome). **Science**, 187, 4182 (Mar. 28, 1975): 1188-1189.

Review of Talcott Parsons and Gerald M. Platt, The American University. **Higher Education** (Amsterdam), 4 (1975): 114-116.

Review of Anatol Rapoport, Conflict in Man-Made Environment. **Journal of Peace Science**, 1, 2 (Spring 1975): 179-181.

Review of Paul Craig Roberts and Mathew A. Stephenson, Marx's Theory of Exchange, Alienation and Crisis (Hoover Institution Studies 36). **Slavic Review**, 34, 2 (June 1975): 406-408.

Review of Thomas Sowell, Say's Law: An Historical Analysis. **Journal of Money, Credit and Banking**, 7, 2 (May 1975): 272-273.

Review of Frederick C. Thayer, An End to Hierarchy! **Journal of Business**, 48, 1 (Jan. 1975): 111-112.

VERSE

Sonnets from the Interior Life and Other Autobiographical Verse. Boulder: Colorado Associated University Press, 1975. 177 pp.

1976

ARTICLES AND PAMPHLET

Adam Smith as an Institutional Economist (pamphlet; Frank E. Seidman Distinguished Award in Political Economy acceptance paper). Memphis, Tenn.: P.K. Seidman Foundation, Nov. 1976. 10 pp. CP VI, pp. 395-406.

Colorado's Kenneth Boulding: A World Renowned Scholar Forecasts Our Future (interview). **Denver Magazine** (July 1976): 47-49, 71-72.

Colorado's Second Century: Outlook and Values. In: **The Colorado Constitution: Is It Adequate for the Next Century?** (report of the Citizens' Assembly on the State Constitution, Boulder, Colo., Aug. 1976). Morrison: Colorado Citizens' Committee on Government, 1976, pp. 8-11.

Comment (on Anita Pfaff, "The Normative Basis of Implicit Grants"). In: **Grants and Exchange** (papers presented at the Joint Institute on Comparative Urban and Grants Economics, Augsburg, Germany, Aug. 1972), Martin Pfaff, ed. Amsterdam: North-Holland Publishing Company, 1976, p. 99.

Comment I (on Margaret J. Gates, "Occupational Segregation and the Law"). **Signs: Journal of Women in Culture and Society,** 1, 3, Part 2 (Spring 1976 Supplement): 75-77. Also in: **Women and the Workplace: The Implications of Occupational Segregation** (based on a conference held at Wellesley, Mass., May 1975), Martha Blaxall and Barbara Reagan, eds. Chicago: University of Chicago Press, 1976, pp. 75-77. RI.

Economics, Evolution, and Law. In: **Law and the American Future**, Murray L. Schwartz, ed. Englewood Cliffs, N.J.: Prentice-Hall, 1976, pp. 30-42.

Economics for Good or Evil. **Technology Review,** 78, 8 (July/Aug. 1976): 5. RI.

Energy and the Environment. Laramie: College of Commerce and Industry, University of Wyoming, Jan. 1976 (Occasional Paper #1). 19 pp.

Equity and Distribution: The Interaction of Markets and Grants. In: **Grants and Exchange** (papers presented at the Joint Institute on Comparative Urban and Grants Economics, Augsburg, Germany, Aug. 1972), Martin Pfaff, ed. Amsterdam: North-Holland Publishing Company, 1976, p. 5-21.

Foreword. In: **Communication Across Cultures for What?** (Symposium on Humane Responsibility in Intercultural Communication), John C. Condon and Mitsuko Saito, eds. Tokyo: Simul Press, 1976, pp. i-iii.

Fruitful Inconsistencies: The Legacy of Adam Smith. **Technology Review,** 78, 5 (Mar./Apr. 1976): 3, 12.

The Great Laws of Change. In: **Evolution, Welfare and Time in Economics: Essays in Honor of Nicholas Georgescu-Roegen** (based on papers presented at the Vanderbilt Centennial Celebration Conference in Honor of Nicholas Georgescu-Roegen, Vanderbilt University, Oct. 1975), Anthony M. Tang, Fred M. Westfield and James S. Worley, eds. Lexington, Mass.: Lexington Books/D.C. Heath Company, 1976, pp. 3-14.

The Importance of Improbable Events. **Technology Review**, 78, 4 (Feb. 1976): 5, 71.

Inflation and the Social Contract. **Technology Review**, 78, 3 (Jan. 1976): 3.

Know-How and the Price of Cheese. **Technology Review**, 78, 7 (June 1976): 5.

Love, Economics, and Mancur Olson. In: **General Systems Theorizing: An Assessment and Prospects for the Future** (Proceedings of the 1976 Annual North American Meeting, Boston, Feb. 1976.) Washington, D.C.: Society for General Systems Research, 1976, pp. 138-143.

The Metaphor is the Message. **Technology Review**, 79, 2 (Dec. 1976): 5.

The Next 200 Years. In: **Finite Resources and the Human Future** (based on papers presented at the Symposium on Global Scarcities, Carleton College, Northfield, Minn., Oct. 1975), Ian G. Barbour, ed. Minneapolis: Augsburg Publishing House, 1976, pp. 155-167.

Outrageous Fortune. **Technology Review**, 79, 1 (Oct./Nov. 1976)· 4-6.

Panel on Food and Development (discussion with others). In: **Finite Resources and the Human Future.** See above.

Panel on Resources and Growth (discussion with others). In: **Finite Resources and the Human Future.** See above.

Panel on the Human Future (discussion with others). In: **Finite Resources and the Human Future.** See above.

Publicly Supported, Universally Available Education and Equality. **Phi Delta Kappan** (special bicentennial issue on Yesterday, Today, and Tomorrow), 58, 1 (Sept. 1976): 36-41.

The Puzzle of the North-South Differential (presented as the Franklin Lecture in the Sciences and Humanities, Auburn University, Apr. 1975). **Southern Humanities Review**, 10, 2 (Spring 1976): 119-130. Also in: **The Southern Mystique: Technology and Human Values in a Changing Region,** W. David Lewis and B. Eugene Griessman, eds. (based on presentations at the Technology and Human Values Conference, Auburn University, Apr. 1975). University: University of Alabama Press, for Auburn University, 1977, pp. 1-13.

Scholarly Rights and Political Morality. In: **Controversies and Decisions: The Social Sciences and Public Policy,** Charles Frankel, ed. New York: Russell Sage Foundation, for the American Academy of Arts and Sciences Project on Social Science Controversies and Public Policy Decisions, 1976, pp. 205-217.

A Sporting Chance. **Technology Review**, 78, 6 (May 1976): 4, 15.

Toward a Theory of Discrimination. In: **Equal Employment Opportunity and the A T & T Case,** Phyllis A. Wallace, ed. Cambridge, Mass.: Massachusetts Institute of Technology Press, 1976, pp. 9-15.

Towards a Sustainable Society: The Transition to Human Maturity. In: **International Symposium on Environment: Toward a Pollution-Free Society** (papers presented at a symposium, Tokyo, May 1976). Tokyo: Nihon Keizai Shimbun (Japan Productivity Center), 1976, pp. 1-11.

Universities in an Evolutionary Environment. In: **The International Association of University Presidents Fourth Conference, Nov. 10-13, 1975,** edited by the Secretariat. Seoul, Korea: Kyung Hee University Press, June 1976, pp. 84-99.

BOOK REVIEWS

Review of Barry Commoner, The Poverty of Power: Energy and the Economic Crisis. **Society,** 14, 1 (Nov./Dec. 1976): 87-89.

Review of Harry G. Johnson, On Economics and Society. **Canadian Journal of Economics,** 9, 2 (May 1976): 385-387.

Review of Matthew Melko, 52 Peaceful Societies. **American Political Science Review,** 70, 1 (Mar. 1976): 206-207.

Review of Saul H. Mendlovitz, ed., On the Creation of a Just World Order: Preferred Worlds for the 1990's. **Journal of Economic Issues,** 10, 3 (Sept. 1976): 720-723.

Review of David Seckler, Thorstein Veblen and the Institutionalists: A Study in the Social Philosophy of Economics. **Land Economics,** 52, 1 (Feb. 1976): 127-128.

Review of Richard T. Selden, ed., Capitalism and Freedom: Problems and Prospects. Proceedings of a Conference in Honor of Milton Friedman. **Journal of Business,** 49, 2 (Apr. 1976): 266-268.

Review of George J. Stigler, The Citizen and the State: Essays on Regulation. **Challenge,** 19, 3 (July/Aug. 1976): 57-58.

Review of Lester Thurow, Generating Inequality: Mechanisms of Distribution in the U.S. Economy; and Stanley Lebergott, The American Economy: Income, Wealth, and Want. **Journal of Economic Issues,** 10, 4 (Dec. 1976): 970-974.

VERSE

Isaac Watts Revised. In: **Finite Resources and the Human Future** (based on papers presented at the Symposium on Global Scarcities, Carleton College, Northfield, Minn., Oct. 1975), Ian G. Barbour, ed. Minneapolis: Augsburg Publishing House, 1976, p. 175.

ALSO OF INTEREST:

Frontiers in Social Thought: Essays in Honor of Kenneth E. Boulding, Martin Pfaff and Janos Horvath, eds. Amsterdam: North-Holland Publishing Company, 1976. viii + 386 pp.

1977

ARTICLES

Adam Smith in the Next Two Hundred Years. In: **Adam Smith and the Wealth of Nations: 1776-1976** (Proceedings of a Bicentennial Conference, Mar. 1976), William R. Morrow and Robert E. Stebbins, eds. Richmond: Eastern Kentucky University, 1977, pp. 724-739.

The American Economic System as an Educator. In: **Beyond the School: What Else Educates?** (report of the Chief State School Officers 1977 Summer Institute, sponsored by the United States Office of Education, in cooperation with the Council of Chief State School Officers and the Michigan Department of Education, Bellaire, Michigan, July/Aug. 1977), Kenneth H. Hansen, ed., pp. 83-91.

The Anxieties of Uncertainty in the Energy Problem. In: **Prospects for Growth: Changing Expectations for the Future,** Kenneth D. Wilson, ed. New York: Praeger Publishers, for Edison Electric Institute, 1977, pp. 114-126. RI.

Commons and Community: The Idea of a Public. In: **Managing the Commons,** Garrett Hardin and John Baden, eds. San Francisco: W.H. Freeman and Company, 1977, pp. 280-294. CP VI, pp. 407-423.

Conversation...with Kenneth E. Boulding (interview). **Organizational Dynamics,** 6, 2 (Autumn 1977): 47-67. RI.

Coping With Decline (summary). **Council of Educational Facility Planners Journal** (report of the 54th Annual Conference, Seattle, Oct. 1977), 15, 6 (Nov./Dec. 1977): 6. Full text distributed as pamphlet: Council of Educational Facility Planners, Columbus, Ohio, 1977. 12 pp.

Determinants of Energy Strategies. In: **Future Strategies for Energy Development: A Question of Scale** (Proceedings of a conference, Oct. 1976). Oak Ridge, Tenn.: Oak Ridge Associated Universities, 1977, pp. 15-33. CP VI, pp. 425-444.

Dialogue (with Wilfred Beckerman; in Japanese) (conducted during the International Economic Association 5th World Congress of Economists, Tokyo, Sept. 1977). **Economist** (Mainichi Newspapers, Tokyo) (Sept. 20, 1977): 10-16.

Energy and the International System. **Mondes en Development** (Paris; special issue on Disarmament and Development), 18 (1977): 237-250.

Energy Policy: A Piece of Cake. **Technology Review,** 80, 2 (Dec. 1977): 8.

The Evolution of Energy. **Cornell Alumni News,** 80, 5 (Dec. 1977): 27-28.

The Free State of Winston: Example or Warning? (discussion of film; with others). In: **The Southern Mystique: The Impact of Technology on Human Values in a Changing Region,** W. David Lewis and B. Eugene Griessman, eds. (based on presentations at the Technology and Human Values Conference, Auburn University, Apr. 1975). University: University of Alabama Press, for Auburn University, 1977, pp. 122-124.

A Friendly Clarification. **Friends Journal**, 23, 18, (Nov. 1, 1977): 552-553. RI.

General Principles, Particular Cases. **Technology Review** 79, 8 (July/Aug. 1977): 4, 80.

Guilt by Association. **Technology Review**, 79, 6 (May 1977): 3.

Less an Experiment Than an Art Form -- An Introduction to the Social Sciences. **Change Magazine** (Report on Teaching: 3), 9, 1 (Jan. 1977): 11. RI.

Looking a Gift Horse in the Mouth. **Technology Review**, 79, 5 (Mar./Apr. 1977): 5.

Metaphors and Models in the International System. In: **Declarations on Principles: A Quest for Universal Peace** ("Liber Amicorum Discipulorumque Prof. B.V.A. Röling"), Robert J. Akkerman, Peter J. Van Krieken, and Charles O. Pannenborg, eds. Leyden: The Netherlands: A.W. Sijthoff, 1977, pp. 311-321.

A National Peace Academy? (letter to the editor). **Washington Post**, June 13, 1977, p. 22.

Notes on Goods, Services, and Cultural Economics. **Journal of Cultural Economics**, 1, 1 (June 1977): 1-14.

The Peace Movement and the Dynamics of Peace (paper presented at the Peace Science Society (Int'l) Southern Section, Lake Cumberland State Park, Kentucky, Apr. 1973). **Peace Progress** (International Association of Educators for World Peace Journal of Education), 1, 4 (1977): 83-87.

Peace Research. **International Social Science Journal**, 29, 4 (special issue on Facets of Interdisciplinarity) (1977): 601-614.

The Power of Nonconflict. **Journal of Social Issues** (special issue on Social Conflict), 33, 1 (Winter 1977): 22-23. CP VI, pp. 445-458.

Prices and Other Institutions. **Journal of Economic Issues**, 11, 4 (Symposium on Contributions to Institutional Economics: Part I) (Dec. 1977): 809-821.

Replacement and Repair: Healing the Body Politic. **Technology Review**, 80, 1 (Oct./Nov. 1977): 5, 23.

Taxes Can Be Fun. **Technology Review**, 79, 7 (June 1977): 4.

This Sporting Life. **Technology Review**, 79, 4 (Feb. 1977): 4-5. RI.

Toward a Normative Science. **Technology Review**, 79, 3 (Jan. 1977): 8, 72.

The Universe as a General System (Fourth Annual Ludwig Von Bertalanffy Memorial Lecture). In: **The General Systems Paradigm: Science of Change of Science** (Proceedings of the 21st Annual North American Meeting, Denver, Feb. 1977). Washington, D.C.: Society for General Systems Research, 1977, pp. 2-7. Reprinted: **Behavioral Science**, 22, 4 (July 1977): 299-306.

The Veracity of Outwardness. **Friends Journal**, 23, 8 (Apr. 15, 1977): 231-232. RI.

Women Employed: Impact on the Family (with others; based on the American Home Economics Association Center for the Family/ J.C. Penney Forum, Boston, June 1977). **Journal of Home Economics**, 69, 5 (Nov. 1977): 14-17.

Wood in the Energy Economy. In: **Forestry for America's Future: Beyond the Bicentennial** (proceedings of the 1976 National Convention). Washington, D.C.: Society of American Foresters, 1977, pp. 1-7.

Yes, Virginia, There Will Be a Year 2000. In: **2000: Tomorrow: Five Perspectives** (Supplement to 1976: United Bank of Denver Annual Review). Denver: United Bank of Denver National Association, 1977, pp. 2-3.

BOOK

The Social System of Planet Earth (with Elise Boulding and Guy M. Burgess; prelim. ed.). Reading, Mass.: Addison-Wesley Publishing Company, 1977. xii + 196 pp. See also: Books, 1980.

BOOK REVIEWS

Review of Cyril S. Belshaw, The Sorcerer's Apprentice: An Anthropology of Public Policy. **Canadian Public Policy**, 3, 1 (Winter 1977): 119.

Review Symposium (with others) of William Breit and William P. Culbertson, Jr., eds., Science and Ceremony: The Institutional Economics of C.E. Ayres. **Journal of Economic Issues**, 11, 3 (Sept. 1977): 657-660.

"Drucker's Pension Fund Socialism," review of Peter F. Drucker, The Unseen Revolution: How Pension Fund Socialism Came to America. **American Banker**, Jan. 31, 1977, pp. 3, 34.

Twelve Friendly Quarrels with Johan Galtung. Review of Johan Galtung, Essays in Peace Research: Vol. 1, Peace Research, Education, Action; Vol. II, Peace, War and Defense. **Journal of Peace Research**, 4, 1 (1977): 75-86. RI.

Review of Irving Louis Horowitz and James Everett Katz, Social Science and Public Policy in the United States. **Journal of Economic Issues**, 11, 3 (Sept. 1977): 702-703.

Review of V.G. Kiernan, Marxism and Imperialism. **American Political Science Review**, 71, 3 (Sept. 1977): 1138-1139.

Review of Assar Lindbeck, Swedish Economic Policy. **Journal of Business**, 50, 2 (Apr. 1977): 248-249.

Review of Howard T. Odum and Elisabeth C. Odum, Energy Basis for Man and Nature. **Friends Journal**, 23, 9 (May 1, 1977): 276-277.

Review of Steven J. Rosen and James R. Kurth, eds., Testing Theories of Economic Imperialism. **American Political Science Review**, 71, 2 (June 1977): 658-660.

Is the "Best" Really Worth It? Review of Tibor Scitovsky, The Joyless Economy: An Inquiry Into Human Satisfaction. **Monthly Labor Review**, 100, 5 (May 1977): 62-63.

VERSE

Summary (of the Conference on Economic Development, Poverty, and Income Distribution, Estes Park, Colo., Apr. 1976). In: **Economic Development, Poverty, and Income Distribution**, William Loehr and John P. Powelson, eds. Boulder, Colo.: Westview Press, 1977, pp. 1, 79, 189.

1978

ARTICLES AND PAMPHLET

Adjusting to Economic Slowdown (in Japanese). **Asahi Journal** (Tokyo), 20, 14 (April 7, 1978): 21-26.

Age Discrimination in an Economic Setting. In: **The Aging in Rural Mid-America: A Symposium on Values for an Evolving Quality of Life** (June 1978), Lloyd Foerster, ed. Lindsborg, Kan.: Bethany College, 1978, pp. 67-77. CP VI, pp. 459-471.

Brief Reflections on the Impact of Science. In: **Proceedings from the National Science Board's Regional Forum: An Experiment with Public Participation in Science Policy Formulation, Feb. 21, 1978.** Denver: American Association of University Women, Colorado State Division, 1978, pp. iv-vi.

Comments (on Roger M. Troub, "Kenneth Boulding: Economics from a Different Perspective," and on Leonard Silk, "The Economics of Kenneth Boulding," papers presented at the Association for Evolutionary Economics Clarence E. Ayres Memorial Session on The Economics of Kenneth Boulding, New York, Dec. 1977). **Journal of Economic Issues**, 12, 2 (June 1978): 535-539.

Dependence and Interdependence as Determinants of Hemispheric Peace (dialogue with Johan Galtung). In: **Conflict, Order, and Peace in the Americas: Part I: Dialogues on the Central Issues,** Norman V. Walbek and Sidney Weintraub, eds. (based on a conference, Nov. 1976). Austin: Lyndon B. Johnson School of Public Affairs, University of Texas, 1978, pp. 87-124.

Dilemmas of the Labour Bargain in the World of the Future (in Dutch). In: **De Toekomst Van Ons Werk,** Geert Hofstede, ed. Leiden: H.E. Stenfert-Kroese B.V., 1978, pp. 81-99. English edition: **Futures for Work: A Book of Original Readings,** Geert Hofstede, ed. (published for the centennial of the first works council in the Netherlands: Nederlandsche Gist-en Spiritusfabriek N.V., 1 November 1878--Gist-Brocades N.V., 1 November 1978). The Hague: Martinus Nijhoff, 1979, pp. 81-98.

Do the Values of Science Lead to a Science of Value? (discussion of George Homans, "What Kind of Myth Is the Myth of a Value-free Social Science?" at the Southwestern Social Science Association, Dallas, Mar. 1977). **Social Science Quarterly**, 58, 4 (Mar. 1978): 548-550.

The Dynamics of World Distribution. In: **Grenzen der Umberteilung,** Martin
Pfaff, ed. (papers presented at the Limits to Redistribution in Stagnating
and in Growing Economies Conference, Augsburg, Germany, July 1976).
Berlin: Duncker & Humblot, 1978, pp. 17-30. CP VI, pp. 473-488.

The Ethic of Science and the E.R.A. **Technology Review,** 80, 8 (Aug./Sept.
1978): 12-13.

Executive Forecast (interview; with others). **Colorado/Business,** 5, 1 (Jan.
1978): 64-65.

Future Directions in Conflict and Peace Studies. **Journal** of **Conflict
Resolution,** 22, 2 (June 1978): 342-354. CP VI, pp. 489-503.

The Future of the Interaction of Knowledge, Energy and Materials. **Behavior
Science Research,** 13, 3 (1978): 169-183.

Grants Economics in the Future of the Financial System (with Thomas Frederick
Wilson). In: **Redistribution Through the Financial System: The Grants
Economics of Money and Credit,** Kenneth E. Boulding and Thomas Frederick
Wilson, eds. (Grants Economics Series). New York: Praeger, 1978, pp. 289-
290.

Has the Wind Turned Against Us? In: **Proceedings of a Symposium on
Implications of Energy Conservation and Supply Alternatives** (Colorado
Springs, Colo., Jan. 1978). East Brunswick, N.J.: Science Applications,
Inc., for the American Chemical Society, 1978, pp. 43-51.

The Household as a Unit in the Social System (with Elise Boulding; 1977-78
Human Ecology Distinguished Lecture, Mar. 1978). **Ecologue** (College of Human
Ecology, Michigan State University, East Lansing), 23, 2 (Fall/Winter
1978): 10-12.

In Praise of Inefficiency (presentation to the Association of Governing Boards
of Universities and Colleges, Denver, Oct. 1977). **AGB Reports,** 20, 1
(Jan./Feb. 1978): 44-48. RI.

An Incomplete Paradigm (reply to Pierre L. van den Berghe, "Sociobiology: A
New Paradigm for the Behavioral Sciences?"). **Social Science Quarterly,** 59,
2 (Sept. 1978): 333-337.

The Legitimacy of the Business Institution. In: **Rationality, Legitimacy,
Responsibility: Search for New Directions in Business and Society,** Edwin M.
Epstein and Dow Votaw, eds. (based on presentations at the General Electric
Foundation's workshop/conference, "Business and Society: State of the Art
and Program for the Future," Berkeley, Calif., Mar. 1975). Santa Monica,
Calif.: Goodyear Publishing Company, 1978, pp. 83-97.

The Limits to Progress in Evolutionary Systems. In: **From Abundance to
Scarcity: Implications for the American Tradition** (The Hammond Lectures:
Number 1; based on lectures given at Ohio State University, Fall 1977).
Columbus: Ohio State University Press, 1978, pp. 17-36. CP VI, pp. 505-
526.

Making Capitalism Just. **Technology Review,** 81, 1 (Oct. 1978): 12-13.

Measure for Measure. **Technology Review,** 80, 5 (Mar./Apr. 1978): 4, 18-19.
RI.

Memoirs of a Pre-Beatle-Liverpudlian-American. **Society,** 15, 3 (Mar./Apr. 1978): 64-73. CP VI, pp. 527-551. RI.

Normative Science and Agricultural Policy (pamphlet; presented as the Fourth James C. Snyder Memorial Lecture in Agricultural Economics, Mar. 1978). West Lafayette, Ind.: Dept. of Agricultural Economics, Purdue University, 1978. 21 pp. RI.

Notes on the Scope of Grants Economics. In: **Association for the Study of the Grants Economy Tenth Anniversary Brochure 1968-1978,** Martin Pfaff, ed. Augsburg, Germany: Center for the Study of the Grants Economy, International Institute for Empirical Social Economics, 1978, pp. 2/2 - 2/4.

Observations on Judgment and Public Policy Decisions. In: **Judgment and Decision in Public Policy Formation,** Kenneth R. Hammond, ed. (AAAS Selected Symposium 1; based on papers presented at the AAAS annual meeting, Denver, Feb. 1977). Boulder, Colo.: Westview Press, for the American Association for the Advancement of Science, 1978, pp. 112-118.

Our Habitat: The Universe. In: **The Future of Human Settlements in the Rocky Mountain West,** Terrell J. Minger, ed. (papers from Vail Symposium VI, Aug. 1976). Vail, Colo.: The Printery at Vail, for the Town of Vail, 1978, pp. 3-12.

Passages: Work and Aging in America. **Technology Review,** 80, 3 (Jan. 1978): 4.

The Power of Negative Thinking. **Technology Review,** 80, 4 (Feb. 1978): 5, 55.

Preface. In: **Redistribution Through the Financial System: The Grants Economics of Money and Credit,** Kenneth E. Boulding and Thomas Frederick Wilson, eds. (Grants Economics Series). New York: Praeger, 1978, pp. v-viii.

Preface. In: **Conflict, Order, and Peace in the Americas: Part 1: Dialogues on The Central Issues,** Norman V. Walbek and Sidney Weintraub, eds. (based on a conference, Nov. 1976). Austin: Lyndon B. Johnson School of Public Affairs, University of Texas, 1978, pp. 1-2.

The Problem of Consensus in American Society. In: **The Search for a Value Consensus** (based on a RF conference, New York, Mar. 1978). New York: Rockefeller Foundation, Sept. 1978, pp. 1-18.

Productivity (with others). **Spectrum** (special issue on Productivity), 15, 10 (Oct. 1978): 41-42, 44.

Reciprocity and Exchange: The Individual and the Household in Society (in French). In: **Les Femmes dans la Société Marchande,** Andrée Michel, ed. (based on presentations at the round table on The Economy and Sociology of the Family, Foundation Royaumont, France, Jan. 1977). Paris: Presses Universitaires de France, 1978, pp. 21-37.

Reflections on Law and Justice (based on a lecture at Cornell University, Oct. 1977). **Cornell Review** (Spring 1978): 11-18. CP VI, pp. 553-562.

Sociobiology or Biosociology? **Society,** 15, 6 (Sept./Oct. 1978): 28-34. Also in: **Sociobiology and Human Nature,** Michael S. Gregory, Anita Silvers, and

Diane Sutch, eds. (based on presentations at the American Association for the Advancement of Science/NEXA Symposium on Sociobiology: Implications for Human Studies, San Francisco State University, June 1977). San Francisco: Jossey-Bass Publishers, 1978, pp. 260-276.

Statement Before the Joint Economic Committee, U.S. Congress. In: **Special Study on Economic Change: Part 3** (Hearings of the Committee, June 1978). Washington, D.C.: U.S. Government Printing Office, 1978, pp. 946-951.

Successes and Failures. **Challenge** (Twentieth Anniversary issue) (Mar./Apr. 1978): 11-13.

Symbol, Substance, and the Moral Economy. **Technology Review**, 81, 2 (Nov. 1978): 4-5. RI.

To Cultivate Our Garden. **Technology Review**, 80, 6 (May 1978): 4.

BOOKS

Ecodynamics: A New Theory of Societal Evolution (A Sage View Edition). Beverly Hills, Calif.: Sage Publications, 1978. 368 pp. Translation: Japanese. Paperback ed. (with study questions), 1981.

Redistribution Through the Financial System: The Grants Economics of Money and Credit (edited with Thomas Frederick Wilson; Grants Economics Series). New York: Praeger Publishers, 1978. xxxiii + 301 pp.

Stable Peace (based on lectures presented while the Distinguished Visiting Tom Slick Professor of World Peace, Lyndon B. Johnson School of Public Affairs, University of Texas, Austin, 1976-77; nominated for a National Book Award, 1979). Austin: University of Texas Press, 1978. xii + 143 pp. Translations: Japanese, Portuguese.

BOOK REVIEWS

Review of Heinz Eulau, Technology and Civility: The Skill Revolution in Politics. **Technology and Culture**, 19, 2 (Apr. 1978): 253-254.

Review of Duncan MacRae, Jr., The Social Function of Social Science. **Journal of Nervous and Mental Disease**, 166, 12 (Dec. 1978): 900-902.

VERSE

A Ballade of Augsburg (written at the German National Science Foundation Symposium: Limits to Distribution in Stagnating and in Growing Economies, Augsburg, June 1976). In: **Association for the Study of the Grants Economy Tenth Anniversary Brochure 1968-1978,** Martin Pfaff, ed. Augsburg, Germany: Center for the Study of the Grants Economy, International Institute for Empirical Social Economics, 1978, pp. 9/3 - 9/8.

Reply (to Fred L. Pryor, "When Boulding Sleeps . . ." In: **Association for the Study of the Grants Economy Tenth Anniversary Brochure 1968-1978,** Martin Pfaff, ed. Augsburg, Germany: Center for the Study of the Grants Economy, International Institute for Empirical Social Economics, 1978, p. 9/9.

1979

ARTICLES AND PAMPHLETS

Appropriate Methodology for Human Learning. In: **Recent Approaches to the Social Sciences,** H.K. Betz, ed. (papers of the Second Symposium, Oct. 1978; Social Sciences Symposium Series, Vol. Two). Calgary, Alberta: Faculty of Social Sciences, University of Calgary, 1979, pp. 181-193.

China Unearths Flowers and Dragons. **Technology Review,** 81, 5 (Mar./Apr. 1979): 8-9.

The City as Teacher and Learner. In: **Housing Perspectives: Individuals and Families,** 2nd ed., Carol S. Wedin and L. Gertrude Nygren, eds. Minneapolis, Minn.: Burgess Publishing Company, 1979, pp. 107-116.

Energy and Social Change. In: **Energy and the Public** (WATTec 6th Annual Energy Conference and Exhibition, Knoxville, Tenn., Feb. 1979). Springfield, Va.: National Technical Information Service, July 1979, pp. 251-259.

Ethics of the Critique of Preferences (lecture presented at the Project on Science and Social Policy, United Campus Ministry, Louisiana State University, Oct. 1976). In: **The Morality of Scarcity: Limited Resources and Social Policy,** William M. Finnin, Jr. and Gerald Alonzo Smith, eds. Baton Rouge: Louisiana State University Press, 1979, pp. 9-23. CP VI, pp. 563-579.

The Evolution of Peace: A Note (based on a lecture at the Peace Science Society (International) meetings, Berlin, Sept. 1979, in conjunction with receiving the Rufus Jones Award of the World Academy of Art and Science). **Man, Environment, Space & Time,** 1, 1 (Fall 1979): 96-97.

Foreword. In: **Conflict Regulation,** by Paul Wehr. Boulder, Colo.: Westview Press, 1979, pp. xiii-xiv.

Gluttoned on Riches or the Beauty of Restraint. **Technology Review,** 81, 3 (Dec. 1978/Jan. 1979): 6, 86.

A Grading Experience. **Technology Review,** 82, 1 (Oct. 1979): 8, 83.

Growth and Progress. In: **Growth in a Finite World,** Joseph Grunfeld, ed. (based on a series of symposia at the Franklin Institute, 1976). Philadelphia: Franklin Institute Press, 1979, pp. 9-20. CP VI, pp. 581-594.

Human Behavior vs. Product Behavior: Comment (on B.N. Ghosh). **Eastern Economic Journal,** 5, 1-2 (Jan./Apr. 1979): 331-332.

In Extremis. **Technology Review,** 81, 8 (Aug./Sept. 1979): 8-9.

Inflation as a Process in Human Learning. In: **Essays in Post-Keynesian Inflation,** James H. Gapinski and Charles E. Rockwood, eds. (based on presentations at the Conference on Inflation held in honor of Abba P.

Lerner, Florida State University, Tallahassee, Mar. 1979). Cambridge, Mass.: Ballinger Publishing Company, 1979, pp. 11-30.

Introduction. In: **The Challenge of Humanistic Economics,** by Mark A. Lutz and Kenneth Lux. Menlo Park, Calif.: Benjamin/Cummings Publishing Company, 1979, pp. v-vii.

The Limits to Societal Growth. In: **Societal Growth: Processes and Implications,** Amos H. Hawley, ed. (based on presentations at the 73rd American Sociological Association annual meeting, San Francisco, Sept. 1978). New York: Free Press, 1979, pp. 317-327.

Malthus the Miserific Vision and the Moral Hope (Third Annual Malthus Lecture, Apr. 1979; pamphlet; Occasional Paper Series 2, 3). Chapel Hill: Institute of Nutrition, University of North Carolina, June 1979. 11 pp.

Managing the Slowdown. **St. Louis Post-Dispatch** (centennial edition on Ideas in Transition: Tomorrow's America), Mar. 25, 1979, pp. 36-39.

The Market and the Budget in Perspective: The Economics of Human Relationships in the Household and in the Society. In: **The Family in Post-Industrial America: Some Fundamental Perceptions for Public Policy Development,** David Pearce Snyder, ed. (based on presentations at a AAAS annual meeting session, Washington, D.C., Jan. 1978; AAAS Selected Symposium 32). Boulder, Colo.: Westview Press, for the American Association for the Advancement of Science, 1979, pp. 5-20.

Marxism and the Future of Capitalism (dialogue with Ernest Mandel, sponsored by the Institute for the Study of Contemporary Social Problems, Seattle, May 1978). **National Forum** (Phi Kappa Phi Journal), 69, 1 (Winter 1979): 18-22.

Measurement in Human Affairs (condensation of paper presented at the American Association for the Advancement of Science annual meeting Symposium on The Metric System: Costs vs. Benefits, Houston, Jan. 1979). **Chemical Engineering,** 57, 5 (Jan. 29, 1979): 5. Complete paper published as: Numbers and Measurement on a Human Scale, 1980.

The Miracle of Japan: How Long Can It Last? In: **Japanese-American Relations in the World Economy** (conference held Aug. 1978). Saratoga Springs, N.Y.: Skidmore College, Spring 1979, pp. 9-37.

Nature and Artifice (based on a presentation at the William O. Douglas Inquiry into the State of Individual Freedom, Washington, D.C., Dec. 1978). **Center Magazine,** 12, 3 (May/June 1979): 2-4.

New Magazine: An Opportunity for the Membership (editorial). **Science,** 206, 4419 (Nov. 9, 1979): 641.

The Next 200 Years: Can We Move Toward a Sustainable High-Level Society? (First Annual World Food Institute Lecture, Apr. 1976; pamphlet). Ames: Iowa State University, 1979. 10 pp.

A Not-So-Simple Little System. **Technology Review,** 82, 2 (Nov. 1979): 8, 85.

A Note on Anatol Rapoport as a Philosopher. In **General Systems: Yearbook of the Society for General Systems Research,** Vol. 23 (1978), Kenneth E. Boulding and H.R. Porter, eds. Louisville, Ky.: System Science Institute,

University of Louisville, for the Society for General Systems Research, 1979, pp. 5-7.

A Note on the Future of Grants Economics. **Association for the Study of the Grants Economy Newsletter,** 10 (Feb. 1979): 2-3.

Numbers Count (condensation of paper presented at the American Association for the Advancement of Science annual meeting Symposium on The Metric System: Costs vs. Benefits, Houston, Jan. 1979). **The Sciences** (New York Academy of Sciences journal), 19, 8 (Oct. 1979): 6-9. Complete paper published as: Numbers and Measurement on a Human Scale, 1980.

The Only Sure Thing About the Future is Uncertainty. In: **Growth in a Conserving Society** (based on papers prepared for the 47th Couchiching Conference of the Canadian Institute of Public Affairs, Geneva Park, Ontario, Aug. 1978). Toronto: Yorkminster Publishing Limited, 1979, pp. 166-172.

Persuading by Threat. **Technology Review,** 81, 4 (Feb. 1979): 10-11.

Philosopher: Ken Boulding (interview). **Christian Science Monitor,** Aug. 7, 1979, pp. B1 - B3. RI.

Pondering the New Decade's Improbables. **Rocky Mountain News** (Denver), Dec. 30, 1979, pp. 43, 58.

Prices and Values: Infinite Worth in a Finite World. In: **Value & Values in Evolution,** Edward A. Maziarz, ed. (based on a paper presented at the Current Evolution of Man's Sense of Values Centenary Symposium, Loyola University, Chicago, Jan. 1970). New York: Gordon and Breach, 1979, pp. 31-46. CP VI, pp. 595-612.

Science and Uncertain Futures. **Technology Review,** 81, 7 (June/July 1979): 8-9.

The Sciences and the Humanities: Kindred Activities (comment). **Humanities Report,** 1, 5 (May 1979): 2-3.

Third Plenary Session: Panel Discussion (with others). In: **The Ethics of Corporate Conduct** (Proceedings of the Twentieth Air Force Academy Assembly, Colorado Springs, Mar. 1978). Englewood Cliffs, N.J.: Prentice-Hall, 1979, pp. 54-80.

The Threatening Economy (with others; by David Mermelstein). **New York Times Magazine,** Dec. 30, 1979, pp. 12-15, 33-34.

Toward a Rethinking of the Quaker Message (based on a paper prepared for a discussion group at Friends General Conference, Ithaca, N.Y., July 1978). **Friends Journal,** 25, 16 (Oct. 1, 1979): 5-8.

The War Industry. In: **Inflation and National Survival,** Clarence C. Walton, ed. (Proceedings of the Academy of Political Science, 33, 3; Proceedings of a conference, Williamsburg, Va., Feb. 1979). New York: Academy of Political Science, in conjunction with the American Council of Life Insurance, 1979, pp. 91-100. CP VI, pp. 613-624.

Welcome. In: **Federal R&D/R&D, Industry, & the Economy: International Aspects of R&D,** Don I. Phillips, Gail J. Breslow, Patricia S. Curlin, eds.

(Colloquium Proceedings, 19-20, June 1979; AAAS Report No. 79-R-14). Washington, D.C.: American Association for the Advancement of Science, for the AAAS Committee on Science, Engineering, and Public Policy, Oct. 1979, pp. 5-6.

Welding and Nondestructive Testing of Social Systems. **Technology Review**, 81, 6 (May 1979): 8-9.

Where Do We Go From Here? -- Reflections on Possible Futures (in Japanese). Tokyo: **The Asahi Shimbun** (Mar.-May 1979), serially in 24 segments.

BOOK

General Systems: Yearbook of the Society for General Systems Research, Vol. XXIII, 1978 (edited with H. R. Porter; published in honor of Anatol Rapoport). Louisville, Ky.: System Science Institute, University of Louisville, for the Society for General Systems Research, 1979. ii + 191 pp.

BOOK REVIEWS

Review of David Collard, Altruism and Economy: A Study in Non-Selfish Economics. **Journal of Political Economy**, 87, 6 (Dec. 1979): 1383-1384.

Heaps and Humps: Why Something Seems Wrong with Everything. Review of Charles E. Lindblom, Politics and Markets: The World's Political-Economic Systems; and Edward R. Tufte, Political Control of the Economy. **Wharton Magazine**, 3, 3 (Spring 1979): 68-69.

Universal Physiology. Review of James Grier Miller, Living Systems. **Contemporary Sociology**, 8, 5 (Sept. 1979): 687-691. RI.

Review of Frederic L. Pryor, The Origins of the Economy: A Comparative Study of Distribution in Primitive and Peasant Economies; and A. Allan Schmid, Property, Power, and Public Choice: An Inquiry Into Law and Economics. **Journal of Economic Issues**, 13, 3 (Sept. 1979): 781-785.

Asking Tough Questions About Rich and Poor Countries. Review of Barbara Ward, Progress for a Small Planet. **Christian Science Monitor**, Nov. 7, 1979, p. 19.

VERSE

Thoughts at the AAAS Workshop on the Role of Scientific and Engineering Societies in Development. In: **The Role of Scientific & Engineering Societies in Development** (Proceedings of a Workshop conducted by the AAAS for the U.S. Department of State, Washington, D.C., May 1979), Jeannette Wedel, ed. Washington, D.C.: American Association for the Advancement of Science, 1979, p. iii.

Verse from the WATTec 6th Annual Energy Conference and Exhibition. In: **Energy and the Public** (WATTec 6th Annual Energy Conference and Exhibition, Knoxville, Tenn., Feb. 1979). Springfield, Va.: National Technical Information Service, July 1979, p. 233.

1980

ARTICLES

The Catastrophe That Wasn't. **Technology Review,** 83, 2 (Nov./Dec. 1980): 4, 76.

Corporate Taxation (letter to the editor with others; comments on Alan F. Kay, "A Less Taxing Way to Pay Uncle Sam"). **Harvard Business Review,** 58, 4 (July/Aug. 1980): 183.

The Economic Background for the Future of Solar Energy. In: **Economics of Solar Energy and Conservation Systems,** Vol. II: **Solar Applications and Cost,** Frank Kreith and Ronald E. West, eds. Boca Raton, Fla.: CRC Press, 1980, pp. 1-6.

Economics in Disarray. **Technology Review,** 82, 6 (May 1980): 6, 20.

Equilibrium, Entropy, Development, and Autopoiesis: Towards a Disequilibrium Economics (paper presented at the American Economic Association annual meeting session on Disequilibrium Economics and, the Evolutionary Vision, Denver, Sept. 1980). **Eastern Economic Journal,** 6, 3-4 (Aug./Oct. 1980): 179-188.

An Evolutionary View of Technology Forecasting. **Technology Review,** 82, 3 (Dec./Jan. 1980): 8-9.

Foreword. In: Emile Benoit, **Progress and Survival: An Essay on the Future of Mankind,** Jack Benoit Gohn, ed. New York: Praeger Publishers, 1980, pp. v-vi.

Foreword. In: **Holonomy: A Human Systems Theory,** by Jeffrey S. Stamps. Seaside, Calif.: Intersystems Publications, 1980, p. i.

Foreword. In: **Subsidies to Higher Education: The Issues,** Howard P. Tuckman and Edward Whalen, eds. New York: Praeger Publishers, 1980, pp. v-vii.

Foreword. In: **Autopoiesis, Dissipative Structures, and Spontaneous Social Orders,** Milan Zeleny, ed. (AAAS Selected Symposium 55). Boulder, Colo.: Westview Press, for the American Association for the Advancement of Science, 1980, pp. xvii-xxi.

Future Cities and Industry: Human Skill Must Outmatch Exhaustion of Resources (paper presented at the Symposium on Cities and Industry in the 21st Century, Kobe, Japan, Feb. 1980). **Japan Economic Journal** (Tokyo), 18, 894 (Mar. 11, 1980): 20, 14.

General Comments. In: **Energy in Transition 1985-2010: Final Report of the Committee on Nuclear and Alternative Energy Systems** (National Research Council, National Academy of Sciences, Washington, D.C., 1979). San Francisco: W.H. Freeman and Company, 1980, pp. 613-618.

The Global Lifeboat: Energy and the Third World. In: **Energy and the Way We Live** (article booklet for the Twelfth Course by Newspaper). San

Francisco: Boyd & Fraser Publishing Company, for Courses by Newspaper, 1980, pp. 25-27.

Graduate Education as Ritual and Substance. In: **Philosophy and Future of Graduate Education,** William K. Frankena, ed. (papers and commentaries presented at an international conference, Apr. 1978). Ann Arbor: University of Michigan Press, 1980, pp. 143-159. CP VI, pp. 625-643.

How to Approach the Future (in Japanese). In: **Visions Towards 80s,** Katsuhisa Yamada, ed. Tokyo: Japanese Government Ministry of International Trade and Industry, 1980.

The Human Mind as a Set of Epistemological Fields (paper presented at the Symposium on Intellect and Imagination: The Limits and Presuppositions of Intellectual Inquiry, Emory University, Atlanta, Oct. 1979). **Bulletin of the American Academy of Arts and Sciences,** 33, 8 (May 1980): 14-30.

The Implications of Improved Water Allocation Policy. In: **Western Water Resources: Coming Problems and the Policy Alternatives** (Federal Reserve Bank of Kansas City Symposium, Denver, Sept. 1979). Boulder, Colo.: Westview Press, 1980, pp. 299-311.

Is Blood Thicker Than Water? **Technology Review,** 83, 1 (Oct. 1980): 6-7.

Money Market Madness. **Technology Review,** 82, 4 (Feb. 1980): 6-7.

The Moral Environment of Public Policy. In: **Increasing Understanding of Public Problems and Policies -- 1980** (Proceedings of the 30th National Public Policy Education Conference, Vail, Colo., Sept. 1980). Oak Brook, Ill.: Farm Foundation, 1980, pp. 3-13.

The Next 100 Years? **Science** (Centennial Issue), 29, 4452 (July 4, 1980): 19. RI.

Numbers and Measurement on a Human Scale. In: **The Metric Debate,** David F. Bartlett, ed. (based on papers presented at the American Association for the Advancement of Science annual meeting, Houston, Jan. 1979). Boulder: Colorado Associated University Press, 1980, pp. 53-66.

On Being Rich and Being Poor: Technology and Productivity. In: **Appropriate Technology and Social Values -- A Critical Appraisal,** Franklin A. Long and Alexandra Oleson, eds. Cambridge, Mass.: Ballinger Publishing Company, in association with the American Academy of Arts and Sciences, 1980, pp. 193-205. CP VI, pp. 645-659.

Physiology and Ecology: The Two Legs of General Systems. In: **Systems Science and Science** (Proceedings of the 24th Annual North American Meeting, with the American Association for the Advancement of Science, San Francisco, Jan. 1980), Bela H. Banathy, ed. Louisville: Society for General Systems Research, Systems Science Institute, University of Louisville, 1980, pp. 178-184.

Preface. In: **Getting Grants,** by Craig W. Smith and Eric W. Skjei. New York: Harper & Row, 1980, pp. xiii-xiv.

The Ripening Society. **Technology Review,** 82, 7 (June/July 1980): 6-7.

Science: Our Common Heritage (presidential address to the American Association for the Advancement of Science annual meeting, San Francisco, Jan. 1980). **Science,** 207, 4433 (Feb. 22, 1980): 831-836. CP VI, pp. 661-681. RI.

Science: A World Community (based on a statement prepared for the American Association for the Advancement of Science International Consortium meeting, Washington, D.C., Feb. 1980). **Chemical and Engineering News,** 58, 15 (Apr. 14, 1980): 3.

Spaceship Earth Revisited. In: **Economics, Ecology, Ethics: Essays Toward a Steady-State Economy,** Herman E. Daly, ed. San Francisco: W.H. Freeman and Company, 1980, pp. 264-266 (with reprint of "The Economics of the Coming Spaceship Earth," 1966).

Statement Before the House Committee on Science and Technology, U.S. Congress. In: **National Academy of Sciences Report: Energy in Transition, 1985-2010** (Hearing of the Committee, Jan. 1980). Washington, D.C.: U.S. Government Printing Office, 1980, pp. 23-26.

Toward a Vintage Society. **Technology Review,** 82, 8 (Aug./Sept. 1980): 4-5.

The Wages of Sin. **Technology Review,** 82, 5 (Mar./Apr. 1980): 6, 20.

Welcome to Our Annual Meeting. In: **American Association for the Advancement of Science Annual Meeting Program: Science: Our Common Heritage,** Arthur Herschman, ed. (San Francisco, Jan. 1980). Washington, D.C.: AAAS, 1980, inside front cover.

BOOKS

Beasts, Ballads, and Bouldingisms: A Collection of Writings by Kenneth E. Boulding, Richard P. Beilock, ed. New Brunswick and London: Transaction Books, 1980. 199 pp.

The Social System of the Planet Earth (with Elise Boulding and Guy M. Burgess). Reading, Mass.: Addison-Wesley Publishing Company, 1980. xvii + 233 pp. Instructor's Manual also. See also: Book, 1977.

BOOK REVIEWS

Review of Roger Benjamin, The Limits of Politics: Collective Goods and Political Change in Postindustrial Societies. **Political Science Quarterly,** 95, 4 (Winter 1980-81): 697-698.

Review of Nicholas Rescher, Scientific Progress: A Philosophical Essay on the Economics of Research in Natural Science. **International Journal of General Systems,** 6, 3 (1980): 173-174.

Yes, the World is Winding Down, But Is the Sky Really Falling, Too? Review of Jeremy Rifkin, Entropy: A New World View. **Christian Science Monitor** (Monthly Book Review Section), Nov. 10, 1980, pp. B4 - B5.

ALSO OF INTEREST

Kenneth Boulding: Economist, Pacifist, Dreamer, by Patricia Kent Gilmore. **Denver Post,** April 13, 1980, pp. 26-27.

1981

ARTICLES

Agricultural Economics in an Evolutionary Perspective. **American Journal of Agricultural Economics,** 63, 5 (Dec. 1981) (Proceedings of the American Agricultural Economics Association annual meeting, Clemson, S.C., July 1981): 788-795.

Allocation and Distribution -- The Quarrelsome Twins (paper presented at the Association for Social Economics annual meeting, Denver, Sept. 1980). In: **Value Judgment and Income Distribution,** Robert A. Solo and Charles W. Anderson, eds. (Praeger Studies in Grants Economics). New York: Praeger Publishers, 1981, pp. 141-164.

Bargaining for What? **Technology Review,** 84, 2 (Nov./Dec. 1981): 4, 20.

Cartels, Prices, and the Grants Economy. In: **The Challenge of the New International Economic Order,** Edwin P. Reubens, ed. (presentations at a conference, City College, N.Y., Apr. 1979). Boulder, Colo.: Westview Press, 1981, pp. 61-70.

Cowboy Economics. **Technology Review,** 83, 6 (May/June 1981): 6-7.

Defending Whom From What? **Technology Review,** 83, 7 (July 1981): 6-7.

The Echo Stops Here. **Technology Review,** 84, 1 (Oct. 1981): 4, 14.

Ecodynamics, A Response by the Author. **Journal of Social and Biological Structures,** 4 (1981): 187-194. (Included in "Kenneth Boulding's **Ecodynamics:** A Symposium on **Ecodynamics: A New Theory of Societal Evolution,**" pp. 145-194).

Economist Drops GOP Affiliation (letter to the editor/to President Reagan). **Boulder Daily Camera,** April 19, 1981, p. 10. See also: Defending Whom From What? 1981. RI.

Escape from Entropy. In: **A New Pattern for Understanding Economics: The Entropy Paradigm** (proceedings of a conference, April 1980). Glassboro, N.J.: Glassboro State College, 1981, pp. 51-55.

The Ethical Background of the Problems of Energy and Food (based on a paper presented at the Conference on Energy and Food, Ohio State University, Oct. 1980). **NICM Journal** (National Institute of Campus Ministries), 6, 2 (Spring 1981): 25-33.

The Evolution of Peace (presentation at the International Congress of Arts and Sciences of the World University of the World Academy of Arts and Science,

Harvard University, Cambridge, Mass., June 1980). **Man, Environment, Space and Time**, 1, 2 (Spring 1981): 77-87.

Faculty Retirement as an Economic and Political Problem (paper presented at the 1981 American Association for Higher Education National Conference, Washington, D.C., Mar. 1981). **AAHE Bulletin**, 33, 9 (May 1981): 1, 12-15. RI.

Foreword. In: **The Evolutionary Vision: Toward a Unifying Paradigm of Physical, Biological, and Sociocultural Evolution**, Erich Jantsch, ed. (AAAS Selected Symposium 61). Boulder, Colo.: Westview Press, for the American Association for the Advancement of Science, 1981, pp. xv-xvi.

Foreword. In: **Choice Over Chance: Economic and Energy Options for the Future**, by William F. Thompson, Jerome J. Karaganis, and Kenneth D. Wilson. New York: Praeger Publishers, for Edison Electric Institute, 1981, pp. v-xii.

Foreword. In: William Welch, **The Art of Political Thinking: Government and Common Sense**, Katharine S. Welch, ed. Totowa, N.J.: Littlefield, Adams and Company, 1981, pp. ix-x.

Foreword. In: **Autopoiesis: A Theory of Living Organization**, Milan Zeleny, ed. (N.H. Series in General Systems Research, Vol. 3). New York: North Holland, 1981, pp. xi-xiii.

Friends and the Economy (presentation to the Friends Committee on National Legislation Dialogue, Guilford College, Greensboro, N.C., Oct. 1980). **Guilford Review**, 13 (Spring 1981): 53-57.

The Future of General Systems. In: **Interdisciplinary Teaching**, Alvin M. White, ed. (New Directions for Teaching and Learning, Number 8). San Francisco: Jossey-Bass, Dec. 1981, pp. 27-34.

Human Knowledge as a Special System (paper prepared for the Society for General Systems Research Silver Anniversary International Meeting, London, Aug. 1979). **Behavioral Science**, 26, 2 (April 1981): 93-102. RI.

Mature People in a Mature Society. In: **Energy and the Elderly: A Public Policy Response**, Patsy J. Daniels, ed. (Conference Proceedings, May 1981). Omaha: The Gerontology Program, College of Public Affairs and Community Service, University of Nebraska at Omaha, 1981, pp. 1-22.

The Meaning of Development. **Technology Review**, 83, 3 (Jan. 1981): 6-7. RI.

On the Virtues of Muddling Through. **Technology Review**, 83, 4 (Feb./Mar. 1981): 6-7.

The Political Paradox. **Technology Review**, 83, 5 (Apr. 1981): 6-7.

Science and Its Social Environment. **Bulletin of Science, Technology and Society**, 1 (1981): 33-35.

Space as a Factor of Production (Wallace W. Atwood Lecture, Apr. 1981). **Monadnock** (Clark University, Worcester, Mass.), Vols. 54 and 55 (1980 and 1981): 15-26.

Survival at Gunpoint. **Technology Review**, 83, 8 (Aug./Sept. 1981): 6-7.

Technology in the Perspective of Societal Evolution (in German).   In: **Fortschritt ohne Maß?: Eine Ortsbestimmung der wissenschaftlichtechnischen Zivilisation,** Reinhard Löw, Peter Koslowski, Philipp Kreuzer, eds. (papers presented at the CIVITAS Symposium on Technological Development -- Progress or Cul-de-sac?, Tegernsee, Germany, May 1980). Munich: R. Piper & Company Verlag, 1981, pp. 168-181.

Toward an Evolutionary Theology. In: **The Spirit of the Earth,** Jerome Perlinski, ed. (A Teilhard Centennial Celebration). New York: Seabury Press, 1981, pp. 105-116.

The World Community of Scholars: Reflections on the Delhi Global Seminar of December 1980. **Scientific and Engineering Societies in Development Newsletter** (American Association for the Advancement of Science), 1 (Fall 1981): 7-8.

BOOKS

Ecodynamics: A New Theory of Societal Evolution.   Paperback edition (including study questions): Beverly Hills, Calif.: Sage Publications, 1981. 368 pp. See also: Books, 1978.

Evolutionary Economics. Beverly Hills, Calif.: Sage Publications, 1981. 200 pp.

A Preface to Grants Economics: The Economy of Love and Fear (Praeger Studies in Grants Economics). New York: Praeger Publishers, 1981. ix + 145 pp.

BOOK REVIEWS

Review of Paul Blumberg, Inequality in an Age of Decline. **Political Science Quarterly,** 96, 2 (Summer 1981): 321-323.

Review of Herman Kahn, World Economic Development: 1979 and Beyond. **Economic Development and Cultural Change,** 29, 3 (Apr. 1981): 645-649.

. . . and when the cupboard is bare? Review of Jerrold H. Krenz, Energy: From Opulence to Sufficiency; and Richard J. Barnet, The Lean Years: Politics in the Age of Scarcity. **Nature,** 289, 5795 (Jan. 1981): 331.

VERSE

A Small Hymn to Science. In: **Report on the Global Seminar on the Role of Scientific and Engineering Societies in Development, New Delhi, December 1-5, 1980.** New Delhi: Indian National Science Academy, in cooperation with the American Association for the Advancement of Science and the Indian Science Congress Association, 1981, p. iii. Also in: **Proceedings of the Global Seminar on the Role of Scientific & Engineering Societies in Development.** New Delhi: Indian National Science Academy, 1982, p. iii.

Sonnets from Laxenburg: On the Numbers From Zero to Ten (written during a visit to the IIASA System and Decision Sciences Area, June/July 1981; pamphlet). Laxenburg, Austria: International Institute for Applied Systems Analysis, 1981. 15 pp.

1982

ARTICLES

Appropriate Strength. **Technology Review**, 85, 2 (Feb./Mar. 1982): 8, 18.

Development as Evolution Towards Human Betterment: How To Go From Bad to Better Instead Of From Bad To Worse (Charles Carter Lectures 1982; pamphlet). Lancaster, England: University of Lancaster, 1982. 47 pp.

Economic Affluence and the Quality of Life. In: **Prospects for Man: The Quality of Life**, W.J. Megaw, ed. (Proceedings of the 5th Annual Prospects for Man Symposium, June 1975). Toronto: Centre for Research on Environmental Quality, Faculty of Science, York University, 1982, pp. 79-87; discussion, pp. 88-95.

Foreword. In: **The Political Economy of Arms Reduction: Reversing Economic Decay**, Lloyd Dumas, ed. (AAAS Selected Symposium 80). Boulder, Colo.: Westview Press, for the American Association for the Advancement of Science, 1982, pp. xiii-xiv.

Foreword. In: **The Logic of Organization: A System-Based Social Science Framework for Organization**, by Alfred Kuhn and Robert D. Beam. San Francisco: Jossey-Bass Publishers, 1982, pp. xi-xii.

Innovation and the Grants Economy. In: **Managing Innovation: The Social Dimensions of Creativity, Invention and Technology** (based on presentations at the Aspen Institute Conference on Creativity, Queenstown, Md., Nov. 1980), Sven B. Lundstedt and E. William Colglazier, Jr., eds. New York: Pergamon Press, with the Aspen Institute for Humanistic Studies and the Ohio State University, 1982, pp. 45-52.

International Economic Relations. In: **Population and the World Economy in the Twenty-First Century**, Just Faaland, ed. (papers presented at the Nobel Symposium on Population Growth and World Economic Development, Noresund, Norway, Sept. 1981). Oxford, England: Basil Blackwell Publisher Ltd., for the Norwegian Nobel Institute, 1982, pp. 128-146; discussion, pp. 147-174.

Interview (with Kyoko Baba; in Japanese). In: **Preparing for the New Era of Internationalized Business.** Tokyo: Kodansha International, 1982, pp. 70-76.

Irreducible Uncertainties (presentation at the American Association for the Advancement of Science annual meeting Symposium on Common Foundations of Economics and Ecology, Washington, D.C., Jan. 1982). **Transaction/Society**, 20, 1 (Nov./Dec. 1982): 11-17.

Kenneth Boulding: A Discussion (with Harry Redner; Part I). **Social Alternatives** (Brisbane, Australia), 3, 1 (Oct. 1982): 15-20. (For Part II, see 1983.)

A New Face for the Democratic Party? **Technology Review**, 85, 3 (Apr. 1982): 8-9.

Pathologies of the Public Grants Economy. In: **The Grants Economy and Collective Consumption**, R.C.O. Matthews and G.B. Stafford, eds. (Proceedings of the International Economic Association Conference, Cambridge, England, Sept. 1979). London: Macmillan Press, for the International Economic Association, 1982, pp. 3-19; discussion, pp. 20-22.

Property: Whose Right? **Technology Review**, 85, 8 (Nov./Dec. 1982): 11, 83.

Rags, Riches, and Redistribution. **New Jersey Bell Journal**, 5, 1 (Spring 1982): 28-34.

The Role of Government in a Free Economy. **Review of Social Economy**, 40, 3 (Dec. 1982) (Proceedings of the Centennial Conference on Economics and Ethics: Retrospect and Prospect, Marquette University, Milwaukee, Wis., Nov. 1981): 417-426.

The Role of Government in a Free Society. **Technology Review**, 85, 6 (Aug./Sept. 1982): 6-7.

The Role of Households in World Development (papers presented at a conference, Oct. 1981; pamphlet). Guelph, Ontario, Canada: College of Family and Consumer Studies, University of Guelph, 1982. 21 pp.

Science and National Defense: A Speculative Essay and Discussion. In: **Science, Technology, and the Issues of the Eighties: Policy Outlook**, Albert H. Teich and Ray Thornton, eds. (report prepared for the National Science Foundation in support of the Second Five Year Outlook for Science and Technology; based on papers presented at two workshops convened by AAAS, Nov./Dec. 1980). Boulder, Colo.: Westview Press, for the American Association for the Advancement of Science, 1982, pp. 253-268.

Science, Technology, and Our Environment (in Japanese; paper presented at the Asahi Shimbun International Symposium on Science and Man, Tokyo, Apr. 1982). Tokyo: The Asahi Shimbun, 1982.

A Second Look at **Progress and Poverty**. In: **Land Value Taxation: The Progress and Poverty Centenary**, Richard W. Lindholm and Arthur D. Lynn, Jr., eds. (Proceedings of the Lincoln Institute of Land Policy Symposium, Cambridge, Mass., Sept. 1978). Madison: University of Wisconsin Press, for the Committee on Taxation, Resources and Economic Development (TRED), 1982, pp. 5-17.

The Social Sciences and Human Development. In: **Proceedings of the Global Seminar on the Role of Scientific and Engineering Societies in Development** (New Delhi, Dec. 1980). New Delhi: The Indian National Science Academy, in cooperation with the American Association for the Advancement of Science and the Indian Science Congress Association, 1982, pp. 36-40.

Undoing Doomsday. **Technology Review**, 85, 4 (May/June 1982): 8, 84.

The Unimportance of Energy. In: **Energetics and Systems**, William J. Mitsch, Rammohan K. Rayode, Robert W. Basserman, and John A. Dillon, Jr., eds. (based on papers presented at the International Society for Ecological Modelling and the Southeast Region of the Society for General Systems Research joint symposium, Louisville, Ky., Apr. 1981). Ann Arbor, Mich.: Ann Arbor Science Publishers, 1982, pp. 101-108.

What Hope for Peace? (in Japanese). **Sekai** (Tokyo) (special issue on Voice for Peace) (July 1982): 68-71.

BOOK REVIEWS

Review of Peter Checkland, Systems Thinking, Systems Practice. **Journal of Applied Systems Analysis,** 9 (1982): 137-138.

Review of Robert Riddell, Ecodevelopment: Economics, Ecology and Development: An Alternative to Growth Imperative Models. **Journal of Economic Literature,** 20, 3 (Sept. 1982): 1076-1077.

Knowledge, Resources, and the Future. Review of Julian L. Simon, The Ultimate Resource; and of Lester R. Brown, Building a Sustainable Society. **Bioscience,** 32, 5 (May 1982): 343-344.

VERSE

Minutes and Comments (Symposium on Colorado Futures, July 1982). **Academy Notes** (Academy of Independent Scholars, Boulder, Colo.), 1, 3 (Sept. 1982): 1.

1983

ARTICLES AND PAMPHLET

Commentary. In: **Free Enterprise: 15 Commentaries,** Bert Elwert, ed. Chicago: College of Business Administration, University of Illinois at Chicago, 1983, pp. 1-4.

The Concept of Evolution in the Interaction Between Science and Religion. In: **Teilhard and the Unity of Knowledge** (Georgetown University Centennial Symposium, May 1981), Thomas M. King and James F. Salmon, eds. New York: Paulist Press, 1983, pp. 57-71; discussion, pp. 72-73.

Conflict Management as a New Discipline. In: **Conflict Resolution Technology,** Donald W. Cole, ed. Cleveland: The Organization Development Institute, 1983, pp. 65-73.

Development as Evolution Towards Human Betterment: How to Go From Bad to Better Instead of From Bad to Worse (Charles Carter Lectures, Nov. 1982). Lancaster, England: University of Lancaster, 1983. 47 pp.

Efficiency and Effectiveness: Normative Foundations of Transfer Policy. In: **Public Transfers and Some Private Alternatives During the Recession** (papers presented at an International Scientific Conference of the Deutsche Forschungsgemeinschaft, Augsburg, Germany, July 1980), Martin Pfaff, ed. Berlin: Duncker & Humblot, for the International Institute for Empirical Social Economics, 1983, pp. 7-21.

The Evolution of Riches. **Science Digest,** 91, 6 (June 1983): 32, 34-35.

Foreword (with Lawrence Senesh). In: **The Optimum Utilization of Knowledge: Making Knowledge Serve Human Betterment,** Kenneth E. Boulding and Lawrence Senesh, eds. (Academy of Independent Scholars Forum Series) (papers presented at the AIS symposium, University of Massachusetts, Amherst, Nov. 1981). Boulder, Colo.: Westview Press, 1983, pp. ix-xi.

Foreword. In: **The Art of Judgment: A Study of Policy Making,** by Sir Geoffrey Vickers. London: Harper & Row Limited, 1983, pp. 7-8 (book orig. pub. 1965).

Hope For The Future: Is War Becoming Obsolete? (conversation with Eugene M. Lang, following the Symposium on Hope for the Future, Apr. 1983). **Swarthmore College Bulletin** (Sept. 1983): 5-6.

How Do Things Go From Bad to Better? The Search for Normative Analysis. **Social Science Journal,** 20, 3 (July 1983) (Western Social Science Association Silver Anniversary: Transformations in the Social Sciences, Albuquerque, Apr. 1983): 9-14.

Illusion of "National Defense." **The Colgate News** (Colgate University), Nov. 11, 1983, p. 8.

Impact Assessment of National Defense. **Impact Assessment Bulletin** (special issue on Impacts of the Arms Race), 2, 4 (Fall 1983): 13-20.

The Information Society. In: **The Princeton Papers: Multinational Management in the Electronic Era** (presentations at the Senior Management Conference, Princeton, N.J., June 1983). Mississauga, Ontario, Canada: Corporate Relations Department, Northern Telecom Limited, Sept. 1983, pp. 32-33.

Introduction. In: Mark Davidson, **Uncommon Sense: The Life and Thought of Ludwig von Bertalanffy (1901-1972), Father of General Systems Theory.** Los Angeles, J.P. Tarcher, 1983, pp. 17-19.

Kenneth Boulding: A Discussion (with Harry Redner; Part II). **Social Alternatives** (Brisbane, Australia), 3, 2 (Mar. 1983): 26-31. (For Part I, see: Articles, 1982.)

National Defense Through Stable Peace (lectures presented June/July 1981; pamphlet). Laxenburg, Austria: International Institute for Applied Systems Analysis, 1983. 38 pp.

On Dennis Pirages, "The Ecological Perspective and the Social Sciences." **International Studies Quarterly,** 27, 3 (Sept. 1983) (Symposium: A Tribute to Harold and Margaret Sprout): 267-269.

The Optimum Utilization of Knowledge: Some Central Concepts. In: **The Optimum Utilization of Knowledge: Making Knowledge Serve Human Betterment,** Kenneth E. Boulding and Lawrence Senesh, eds. (Academy of Independent Scholars Forum Series) (papers presented at the AIS symposium, University of Massachusetts, Amherst, Nov. 1981). Boulder, Colo.: Westview Press, 1983, pp. 1-19.

Perspectives on Violence. **Zygon,** 18, 4 (Dec. 1983) (special issue on Origins, Functions, and Management of Aggression in Biocultural Evolution; papers presented at an Institute on Religion in an Age of Science symposium, American Association for the Advancement of Science annual meeting, Washington, D.C., Jan. 1982): 425-437.

Quakerism and the Arts (presentation at the Intermountain Yearly Meeting, Ghost Ranch, N.M., June 1983). **Friends Journal**, 29, 16 (Nov. 1, 1983): 5-7.

Reflections on the Uncertain Future of Social and Community Life. In: **Handbook of Social Intervention**, Edward Seidman, ed. Beverly Hills, Calif.: Sage Publications, 1983, pp. 639-651.

Reflections on Values, Science, War and Peace: What Signs of Hope? (address at the 10th General Conference of the International Peace Research Association plenary session on Global Demilitarization, Gyor, Hungary, Sept. 1983). **Bulletin of Peace Proposals**, 14, 4 (1983): 351-354.

Science and the Christian Phylum in Evolutionary Tension. In: **The Experiment of Life: Science and Religion**, F. Kenneth Hare, ed. (papers presented at the William Temple Centenary Conference, Trinity College, Toronto, Aug. 1981). Toronto: University of Toronto Press, 1983, pp. 89-109.

System Theory, Mathematics, and Quantification (comment on Hassan Mortazavian, "System Theory and Its Relevance to Information Science Problems"). In: **The Study of Information: Interdisciplinary Messages**, Fritz Machlup and Una Mansfield, eds. New York: John Wiley & Sons, 1983, pp. 547-550.

Technology in the Evolutionary Process. In: **The Trouble With Technology**, Stuart Macdonald, D. McL. Lamberton, Thomas Mandeville, eds. London: Frances Pinter Publishers, 1983, pp. 4-10.

World Society: The Range of Possible Futures. In: **How Humans Adapt: A Biocultural Odyssey**, Donald J. Ortner, ed. (papers presented at the Seventh International Symposium, Smithsonian Institution, Washington, D.C., Nov. 1981; Smithsonian International Symposia Series). Washington, D.C.: Smithsonian Press, 1983, pp. 395-421.

BOOK

The Optimum Utilization of Knowledge: Making Knowledge Serve Human Betterment (edited with Lawrence Senesh; Academy of Independent Scholars Forum Series) (papers presented at the AIS symposium, University of Massachusetts, Amherst, Nov. 1981). Boulder, Colo.: Westview Press, 1983. xi + 382 pp.

BOOK REVIEWS

Review of Thomas Balogh, The Irrelevance of Conventional Economics. **Journal of Economic Literature**, 21, 2 (June 1983): 554-555.

Ecodynamics. Review of Kenneth E. Boulding, Ecodynamics: A New Theory of Societal Evolution. **Interdisciplinary Science Reviews** (London), 8, 2 (June 1983): 108-113.

Filling in the Niches. Review of Kenneth E. Boulding, Ecodynamics: A New Theory of Societal Evolution. **Science Digest**, 91, 1 (Jan. 1983): 98.

Review of Robert Gilpin, War and Change in World Politics. **Transaction/Society**, 20, 3 (Mar./Apr. 1983): 83-84.

Review of Garrett Hardin, Naked Emperors: Essays of a Taboo-Stalker. **Population and Development Review**, 9, 2 (June 1983): 372-374.

VERSE

Sonnet For Prayer. **Friends Journal**, 29, 6 (Apr. 1, 1983): 11. Also in: **Quaker Life**, 24, 3 (Apr. 1983): 11.

ALSO OF INTEREST

A Man For All Systems: Talking with Kenneth Boulding, by Geoffrey C. Harcourt. **Journal of Post Keynesian Economics**, 6, 1 (Fall 1983): 143-154.

1984

ARTICLES

Changes in Human Valuations Will Eliminate Starvation and Poverty (paper presented at the Asahi Shimbun International Symposium on A Message to the 21st Century, Tokyo, Oct. 1984). **Asahi Evening News** (Tokyo), Oct. 26, 1984, p. 6.

Cybernetics in the Evolutionary Process. In: **Technology, International Stability and Growth** (papers presented at the International Cybernetics Society Conference, Denver, Oct. 1979), S. Basheer Ahmed and Alice Pearce Ahmed, eds. Port Washington, N.Y.: National University Publications, Associated Faculty Press, 1984, pp. 1-14.

The Fallacy of Trends: On Living With Unpredictability. **National Forum** (Phi Kappa Phi Journal), LXIV, 3 (Summer 1984): 19-20.

Foreword. In: **The Economics of Human Betterment** (Proceedings of Section F (Economics) of the British Association for the Advancement of Science annual meeting, University of Sussex, England, Aug. 1983), Kenneth E. Boulding, ed. London: Macmillan Press, 1984, pp. ix-x.

How Do Things Go From Bad to Better?: The Contribution of Economics (presidential address to Section F (Economics). In: **The Economics of Human Betterment**, Kenneth E. Boulding, ed. (Proceedings of Section F, British Association for the Advancement of Science annual meeting, University of Sussex, England, Aug. 1983). London: Macmillan Press 1984, pp. 1-14.

The Meaning of the Twenty-First Century: Reexamining the Great Transition. **World Future Society Bulletin**, 18, 4 (July/August 1984): 1-6.

The Next Thirty Years in General Systems (guest editorial). **General Systems Bulletin**, 15, 1 (Fall 1984): 2-4.

Pathologies of Defense. **Journal of Peace Research**, 21, 2 (1984): 101-108.

Preface (in Spanish). In: Carlos Federico Obreyón Díaz, **De la Filosofía a la Economía: Historia de la Armonía Social.** Mexico City: Editorial Trillas, 1984, pp. 5-7.

Response (to Gibson Winter, "Hope for the Earth: A Nermeneutic of Nuclearism") (with others). **Religion and Intellectual Life,** 1, 3 (Spring 1984): 39-43.

Skinner: A Dissident View (comments on B.F. Skinner, "Selection by Consequences"). **Behavioral and Brain Sciences,** 7, 4 (Dec. 1984): 484.

Sources of Reasonable Hope for the Future. **American Economic Review** (Papers and Proceedings of the 96th American Economic Association annual meeting, San Francisco, Dec. 1983), 74, 2 (May 1984): 221-225.

Statement to the Continuing Committee (presentation to the AAAS Continuing Global Seminar Committee meeting, New Delhi, India, Dec. 1983). **Scientific and Engineering Societies in Development Newsletter** (American Association for the Advancement of Science), 5 (Winter 1984): 5-7.

Toward an Evolutionary Theology. In: **Science and Creationism,** Ashley Montayu, ed. New York: Oxford University Press, 1984, pp. 142-158.

BOOK

The Economics of Human Betterment (edited) (Proceedings of Section F (Economics) of the British Association for the Advancement of Science, annual meeting, University of Sussex, England, Aug. 1983). London, Macmillan Press, 1984. xiii + 220 pp.

BOOK REVIEWS

Review of Robert Axelrod, The Evolution of Cooperation. **Commonweal,** CXI, 10 (May 18, 1984): 310, 314.

Review of Francis A. Beer, Peace Ayainst War: The Ecoloyy of International Violence. **Human Ecology,** 12, 2 (June 1984): 209-213.

Review of Peter G. Elkan, The New Model Economy: Economic Inventions for the Rest of the Century. **Journal of Economic Literature,** 22, 3 (Sept. 1984): 1125-1126.

Review of Hazel Henderson, Creatiny Alternative Futures: The End of Economics. **Journal of Social and Biological Structures,** 7 (1984): 81-83.

Review of Richard R. Nelson and Sidney G. Winter, An Evolutionary Theory of Economic Change. **American Journal of Agricultural Economics,** 66, 4 (Nov. 1984): 535-536.

VERSE

Sonnet (on the creation of an Institute of Peace, by the United States Conyress, Oct. 1984). Washinyton, D.C.: National Peace Academy Campaiyn, Dec. 1984.

ALSO OF INTEREST

Kenneth and Elise Boulding: Partners in Building the New Jerusalem, by Cynthia Kerman and Carlene Bagnall. In: **Living in the Light: Some Quaker Pioneers of the 20th Century,** Leonard S. Kenworthy, ed. Kennett Square, Pa.: Friends General Conference and Quaker Publications, 1984, pp. 22-40.

ARTICLES, MONOGRAPHS, AND PAMPHLETS BY TITLE

Abolition of Membership, 1942
Accomplishments and Prospects of the Peace Research Movement (with
    Hanna and Alan Newcombe), 1968
Adam Smith as an Institutional Economist, 1976
Adam Smith in the Next Two Hundred Years, 1977
Adjusting to Economic Slowdown (in Japanese), 1978
After Samuelson, Who Needs Adam Smith? 1971
Age Discrimination in an Economic Setting, 1978
Agricultural Economics in an Evolutionary Perspective, 1981
Agricultural Organizations and Policies: A Personal Evaluation, 1963
Allocation and Distribution -- The Quarrelsome Twins, 1981
America's Economy: The Qualified Uproarious Success, 1968
America's Great Delusion, 1965
The American Economic System as an Educator, 1977
The American Economy After Vietnam, 1971
The Anxieties of Uncertainty in the Energy Problem, 1977
An Application of Population Analysis to the Automobile Population of
    the United States, 1955
The Application of the Pure Theory of Population Change to the Theory
    of Capital, 1934
Appropriate Methodology for Human Learning, 1979
Appropriate Strength, 1982
Aristocrats Have Always Been Sons of Bitches (interview with Robert W.
    Glasgow), 1973
Arms Limitations and Integrative Activity as Elements in the Establishment
    of Stable Peace, 1966
ASGE--In Retrospect and Prospect, 1973
Asset Identities in Economic Models, 1951

The Background and Structure of a Macro-Economic Theory of Distribution,
    1950
The Balance of Peace, 1970
Bargaining for What? 1981
The Basis of Value Judgments in Economics, 1967
Better R-E-D Than Dead, 1962
Bottleneck Economics, 1974
The Boundaries of Social Policy, 1967
Brief Reflections on the Impact of Science, 1978
Business and Economic Systems, 1968

Can Peace Be Taught?, 1975
Can There Be a Growth Policy? 1973
Can There Be a National Policy for Stable Peace? 1970
Can We Afford a Warless World? 1962
Can We Control Inflation in a Garrison State? 1951
Can We Curb Inflation Without Recession? If So, How? 1970
Capital and Interest, 1960
Cartels, Prices, and the Grants Economy, 1981
The Catastrophe That Wasn't, 1980
The Challenge of Change, 1973
The Challenge of the Great Transition (in Japanese), 1970
Changes in Human Valuations Will Eliminate Starvation and Poverty, 1984
Changes in Physical Phenomena: Discussion (with others), 1956

Defense and Opulence: The Ethics of International Economics, 1951
Demand and Supply, 1968
Democracy and Organization, 1958
Dependence and Interdependence as Determinants of Hemispheric Peace, 1978
Desirable Changes in the National Economy After the War, 1944
Determinants of Energy Strategies, 1977
Development as Evolution Towards Human Betterment: How to Go From Bad to
     Better Instead of From Bad To Worse, 1982
Dialogue (in Kenneth B. Clark, ed., Racism and American Education: A
     Dialogue and Agenda for Action; with others), 1970
Dialogue (with Wilfred Beckerman; in Japanese), 1977
Dialogue (with others; Racism and American Education Conference), 1970
Dialogue--Civilized Society (with John Kenneth Galbraith), 1975
The Difficult Art of Doing Good, 1965
The Dilemma of Power and Legitimacy, 1965
Dilemmas of the Labour Bargain in the World of the Future (in Dutch), 1978;
     (in English), 1979
The Dimensions of Economic Freedom, 1964
Discussion (of Allen V. Kneese, "Environmental Pollution: Economics
     and Policy"), 1971
Divided Views on Tax Increase, 1967
Do the Values of Science Lead to a Science of Value? 1978
The Dodo Didn't Make It: Survival and Betterment, 1971
Doers and Stoppers, 1975
Does Large Scale Enterprise Lower Costs? Discussion (with others), 1948
Does the Absence of Monopoly Power in Agriculture Influence the Stability
     and Level of Farm Income? 1957
The Domestic Implications of Arms Control, 1960
The Doubtful Future, 1974
The Dynamics of Disarmament, 1961
The Dynamics of Society, 1968
The Dynamics of World Distribution, 1978

The Echo Stops Here, 1981
Ecodynamics, A Response by the Author, 1981
ECON is a Four-Letter Word, 1974
Economic Affluence and the Quality of Life, 1982
Economic Analysis and Agricultural Policy, 1947
The Economic Background for the Future of Solar Energy, 1980
The Economic Consequences of Some Recent Antitrust Decisions: Discussion
     (with others), 1949
Economic Education: The Stepchild Too is Father of the Man, 1969
Economic Issues in International Conflict, 1953
Economic Libertarianism, 1965
Economic Progress as a Goal in Economic Life, 1953
Economic Resources and World Peace, 1961
Economic Theory of Natural Liberty, 1973
Economic Theory: The Reconstruction Reconstructed, 1957
Economics, 1965
Economics and Accounting: The Uncongenial Twins, 1962
Economics and Ecology, 1966
The Economics and Financing of Technology in Education: Some Observations,
     1968
Economics and General Systems, 1972
Economics and the Behavioral Sciences: A Desert Frontier? 1956
Economics and the Ecosystem, 1975
Economics as a Moral Science, 1969
Economics as a Not Very Biological Science, 1972

Economics as a Social Science, 1952
Economics, Evolution, and Law, 1976
Economics for Good or Evil, 1976
Economics in Disarray, 1980
The Economics of Ecology, 1973
The Economics of Energy, 1973
The Economics of Human Conflict, 1965
The Economics of Knowledge and the Knowledge of Economics, 1966
The Economics of Reconstruction, 1941
The Economics of the Coming Spaceship Earth, 1966
Economics: The Taming of Mammon, 1956
The Economist and the Engineer: Economic Dynamics of Water Resource
      Development, 1964
Economist Drops GOP Affiliation, 1981
An Economist Looks at the Future of Sociology, 1967
An Economist's View of the Manpower Concept, 1954
Education and the Economic Process, 1969
Education for the Spaceship Earth, 1968
The Effects of Military Expenditure Upon the Economic Growth of Japan
      (edited with Norman Sun), 1968
Efficiency and Effectiveness: Normative Foundations of Transfer Policy,
      1983
Energy and Social Change, 1979
Energy and the Environment, 1976
Energy and the International System, 1977
Energy Policy: A Piece of Cake, 1977
Entropy Economics, 1975
Environment and Economics, 1971
Envisioning the Future (interview), 1975
An Epitaph: The Center for Research on Conflict Resolution, 1959-1971,
      1971
Equality and Conflict, 1973
Equilibrium and Wealth: A Word of Encouragement to Economists, 1939
Equilibrium, Entropy, Development, and Autopoiesis: Towards a
      Disequilibrium Economics, 1980
Equity and Distribution: The Interaction of Markets and Grants, 1976
Escape From Entropy, 1981
The Ethic of Science and the E.R.A., 1978
The Ethical Background of the Problems of Energy and Food, 1981
Ethical Dilemmas in Religion and Nationalism, 1968
The Ethical Perspective, 1962
Ethics and Business: An Economist's View, 1962
Ethics of Growth, 1974
The Ethics of Rational Decision, 1966
Ethics of the Critique of Preferences, 1979
The Evaluation of Large Systems, 1975
Evidences for an Administrative Science, 1958
Evolution and Revolution in the Developmental Process, 1967
The Evolution of Energy, 1977
The Evolution of Peace, 1981
The Evolution of Peace: A Note, 1979
The Evolution of Riches, 1983
The Evolutionary Potential of Quakerism, 1964
An Evolutionary View of Technology Forecasting, 1980
Executive Forecast (interview; with others), 1978
Expecting the Unexpected: The Uncertain Future of Knowledge and
      Technology, 1966
An Experiment in Friendship, 1938

Factors Affecting the Future Demand for Education, 1970
Faculty Retirement as an Economic and Political Problem, 1981
Failures and Successes of Economics, 1969
The Fallacy of Trends: On Living With Unpredictability, 1984
The Family Segment of the National Economy, 1970
The Fifth Meaning of Love--Notes on Christian Ethics and Social
     Policy, 1969
Foreword (in Emile Benoit, Progress and Survival: An Essay on the Future of
     Mankind, Jack Benoit Gohn, ed.), 1980
Foreword (in Kenneth E. Boulding, ed., The Economics of Human Betterment),
     1984
Foreword (in John C. Condon, and Mitsuko Saito, eds., Communicating Across
     Cultures For What?), 1976
Foreword (in Roger M. Downs and David Stea, eds., Image and Environment:
     Cognitive Mapping and Spatial Behavior), 1973
Foreword (in Lloyd Dumas, ed., Political Economy of Arms Reduction:
     Reversing Economic Decay), 1982
Foreword (in Gerhard Hirschfeld, The People: Growth and Survival), 1973
Foreword (in Erich Jantsch, ed., The Evolutionary Vision: Toward a
     Unifying Paradigm of Physical, Biological, and Sociocultural Evolution),
     1981
Foreword (in Cynthia Kerman, Creative Tension: The Life and Thought of
     Kenneth Boulding), 1974
Foreword (in Alfred Kuhn, The Logic of Social Systems), 1974
Foreword (in Alfred Kuhn and Robert D. Beam, The Logic of Organization: A
     System-Based Social Science Framework for Organization), 1982
Foreword (in T.R. Malthus, Population: The First Essay), 1959
Foreword (in Fred Polak, The Image of the Future, Elise Boulding, trans.),
     1973
Foreword (in Jeffrey S. Stamps, Holonomy: A Human Systems Theory), 1980
Foreword (in William F. Thompson et al., Choice Over Chance: Economic and
     Energy Options for the Future), 1981
Foreword (in Howard P. Tuckman and Edward Whalen, eds., Subsidies to Higher
     Education: The Issues), 1980
Foreword (in Sir Geoffrey Vickers, The Art of Judgment: A Study of Policy
     Making), 1983
Foreword (in Paul Wehr, Conflict Regulation), 1979
Foreword (in William Welch, The Art of Political Thinking: Government and
     Common Sense, Katharine Welch, ed.), 1981
Foreword (in Milan Zeleny, ed., Autopoiesis: A Theory of Living
     Organization), 1981
Foreword (in Milan Zeleny, ed., Autopoiesis, Dissipative Structures, and
     Spontaneous Social Orders), 1980
Foreword (with Lawrence Senesh; in Kenneth Boulding and Lawrence Senesh,
     eds., The Optimum Utilization of Knowledge), 1983
The Formation of Values as a Process in Human Learning, 1969

The Free State of Winston: Example or Warning? (discussion; with others),
     1977
A Friendly Clarification, 1977
Friends and Social Change, 1968
Friends and the Economy, 1981
Fruitful Inconsistencies: The Legacy of Adam Smith, 1976
The Fruits of Progress and the Dynamics of Distribution, 1953
Fun and Games with the Gross National Product--The Role of Misleading
     Indicators in Social Policy, 1970
Fundamental Considerations, 1970

The Future as Chance and Design (in German), 1969; (in English), 1974
Future Cities and Industry: Human Skill Must Outmatch Exhaustion of
     Resources, 1980
The Future Corporation and Public Attitudes, 1963
Future Directions (with Martin Pfaff), 1972
Future Directions in Conflict and Peace Studies, 1978
Future Education Pattern at MSC, 1974
The Future of General Systems, 1981
The Future of Personal Responsibility, 1972
The Future of the Interaction of Knowledge, Energy and Materials, 1978
The Future of the Social Sciences, 1965

Gaps Between Developed and Developing Nations, 1970
General Comments (in Energy in Transition 1985-2010), 1980
General Principles, Particular Cases, 1977
General Systems as a Point of View, 1964
General Systems as an Integrating Force in the Social Sciences, 1973
General Systems Theory: The Skeleton of Science, 1956
The Global Lifeboat: Energy and the Third World, 1980
Gluttoned on Riches or the Beauty of Restraint, 1979
A Grading Experience, 1979
Graduate Education as Ritual and Substance, 1980
Grants Economics: A Simple Introduction (with Martin Pfaff and Janos
     Horvath), 1972
Grants Economics in the Future of the Financial System (with Thomas F.
     Wilson), 1978
The Grants Economy, 1969
The Grants Economy and the Development Gap (with Martin Pfaff), 1972
Grants Versus Exchange in the Support of Education, 1968
The Great Laws of Change, 1976
The Great Revolution, 1952
Great Society, or Grandiose? 1965
Greatness as a Pathology of the National Image, 1968
Growth and Progress, 1979
Guilt by Association, 1977

Has the Wind Turned Against Us? 1978
Heretic Among Economists (interview), 1969
The High Price of Technology Misused, 1975
A Historical Note from the President, 1968
The Home as a House of Worship, 1945
Hope for the Future: Is War Becoming Obsolete? 1983
The Household as a Unit in the Social System (with Elise Boulding), 1978
The Household as Achilles' Heel, 1972
How Do Things Go From Bad to Better?: The Contribution of Economics, 1984
How Do Things Go From Bad to Better? The Search for Normative Analysis,
     1983
How Things Go From Bad to Worse, 1972
How Scientists Study "Getting Along," 1965
How to Approach the Future (in Japanese), 1980
Human Behavior vs. Product Behavior: Comment (on B. N. Ghosh), 1979
Human Betterment and the Quality of Life, 1972
Human Knowledge as a Special System, 1981
The Human Mind as a Set of Epistemological Fields, 1980
Human Resources Development as a Learning Process, 1967

Illusion of "National Defense," 1983
Imagining Failure, Successfully, 1974

Impact Assessment of National Defense, 1983
The Impact of the Defense Industry on the Structure of the American
      Economy, 1970
The Impact of the Draft on the Legitimacy of the National State, 1967
Implications for General Economics of More Realistic Theories of the
      Firm, 1952
The Implications of Improved Water Allocation Policy, 1980
The Importance of Improbable Events, 1976
Impressions of the World Conference on Church and Society, 1966
In Defense of Monopoly, 1945
In Defense of Monopoly: Reply, 1946
In Defense of Statics, 1955
In Defense of the Supernatural, 1938
In Extremis, 1979
In Praise of Danger, 1942
In Praise of Inefficiency, 1978
In Praise of Maladjustment, 1939
In Praise of Selfishness, 1940
The Incidence of a Profits Tax, 1944
Income or Welfare? 1950
An Incomplete Paradigm (reply to Pierre L. van den Berghe, "Sociology"), 1978
Industrial Revolution and Urban Dominance: Discussion (with others), 1956
Inflation and the Social Contract, 1976
Inflation as a Process in Human Learning, 1979
The Information Society, 1983
Innovation and the Grants Economy, 1982
Insight and Knowledge in the Development of Stable Peace, 1965
Integrative Aspects of the International System, 1966
An Interdisciplinary Honors Course in General Systems, 1962
International Economic Relations, 1982
The International System in the Eighties: Models of International Peace, 1975
The Interplay of Technology and Values: The Emerging Superculture, 1969
Intersects: The Peculiar Organizations, 1973
Interview (with Kyoko Baba; in Japanese), 1982
Interview: Kenneth E. Boulding (in Economics 73-74), 1973
Interview: Kenneth E. Boulding (in The Study of Society), 1974
An Interview With Kenneth E. Boulding (Seikyo Times), 1971
Introducing Freshmen to the Social System (with Elise Boulding), 1974
Introduction (for A Trans-Atlantic Dialogue; videotape), 1974
Introduction (in Kenneth Boulding and Tapan Mukerjee, eds., Economic
      Imperialism: A Book of Readings), 1972
Introduction (in Mark Davidson, Uncommon Sense: The Life and Thought of
      Ludwig von Bertalanffy), 1983
Introduction (in Clyde Eagleton, Analysis of the Problem of War), 1972
Introduction (in Mark A. Lutz and Kenneth Lux, The Challenge of Humanistic
      Economics), 1979
Introduction (in Mark Rodekohr, Adjustments of Colorado School Districts to
      Declining Enrollments), 1975
Introduction (in Richard G. Wilkinson, Poverty and Progress: An Ecological
      Perspective on Economic Development), 1973
Introduction: Thirsting for the Testable (in Craig Liske et al., eds.,
      Comparative Public Policy) 1975
Introduction to the Global Society: Interdisciplinary Perspectives (with
      Elise Boulding), 1974
An Invitation to Join a New Association for the Study of the Grants Economy,
      1969
The Inward Light, 1947
Irreducible Uncertainties, 1982

Is Blood Thicker Than Water? 1980
Is Economics Culture-Bound? 1970
Is Economics Necessary? 1949
Is It the System or Is It You? 1944
Is Peace Researchable? 1962
Is Scarcity Dead? 1966
Is There a General Theory of Conflict? 1967
Is Ugliness the Price of Prosperity? 1968

Japan Should Produce "Things" With Value Rather Than a "Strong Yen"
    (interview; in Japanese), 1972
The Jungle of Hugeness: The Second Age of the Brontosaurus, 1958
Justifications for Inequality: The Contributions of Economic Theory, 1975

Kenneth Boulding: A Discussion (with Harry Redner; Parts I and II), 1982 and
    1983
Kenneth Boulding: The Arrival of Spaceship Earth (interview), 1972
Kenneth E. Boulding (interview), 1974
Know-How and the Price of Cheese, 1976
Knowledge as a Commodity, 1962
Knowledge as a Road to Peace, 1971
Knowledge as an Economic Variable, 1964
The Knowledge Boom, 1966
The Knowledge Explosion, 1970
The Knowledge of Value and the Value of Knowledge, 1959

Land as a Servant of Man: A Systematic Look at Land Use, 1974
The Learning and Reality-Testing Process in the International System, 1967
The Learning of Peace, 1974
The Learning Process in the Dynamics of Total Societies, 1967
The Legitimacy of Central Banks, 1971
The Legitimacy of Economics, 1967
The Legitimacy of the Business Institution, 1978
The Legitimation of the Market, 1968
Less an Experiment Than an Art Form--An Introduction to the Social Sciences,
    1977
Letter on "Happiness" (in Japanese), 1971
The Liberal Arts Amid a Culture in Crisis, 1972
Limits of the Earth: Discussion (with others), 1956
The Limits to Progress in Evolutionary Systems, 1978
The Limits to Societal Growth, 1979
A Liquidity Preference Theory of Market Prices, 1944
A Look at National Priorities, 1970
A Look at the Corporation, 1957
Looking a Gift Horse in the Mouth, 1977
Looking Ahead to the Year 2000, 1965
Love, Economics, and Mancur Olson, 1976
Love, Fear and the Economist (interview), 1973

Machines, Men and Religion, 1968
Making Capitalism Just, 1978
Making Education Religious, 1938
Malthus the Miserific Vision and the Moral Hope, 1979
The Malthusian Model as a General System, 1955
Man as a Commodity, 1972
Man's Choice: Creative Development or Revolution, 1968
The Management of Decline, 1975
Managing the Slowdown, 1979

The "Mantle of Elijah" Complex, 1972
The Many Failures of Success, 1968
The Market and the Budget in Perspective: The Economics of Human
     Relationships in the Household and in the Society, 1979
Market: Economic Theory, 1964
Marxism and the Future of Capitalism, 1979
Mature People in a Mature Society, 1981
Mayer-Boulding Dialogue on Peace Research, 1967
The Meaning of Development, 1981
The Meaning of Human Betterment, 1971
The Meaning of the Twenty-First Century: Reexamining the Great Transition,
     1984
Measure for Measure, 1978
Measurement in Human Affairs, 1979
Memoirs of a Pre-Beatle-Liverpudlian-American, 1978
A Memorandum on the Facilitation of Behavioral Thinking (with Richard
     Christie), 1969
The Menace of Methuselah: Possible Consequences of Increased Life
     Expectancy, 1965
The Metaphor is the Message, 1976
Metaphors and Models in the International System, 1977
The Miracle of Japan: How Long Can It Last? 1979
The Misallocation of Intellectual Resources, 1963
The Misallocation of Intellectual Resources in Economics, 1971
The Models for a Macro-Economic Theory of Distribution, 1950
Modern Man and Ancient Testimonies, 1969
Money Market Madness, 1980
The Moral Environment of Public Policy, 1980

National Defense Through Stable Peace, 1983
National Images and International Systems, 1959
The "National" Importance of Human Capital, 1968
A National Peace Academy? 1977
Nationalism, Millennialism and the Quaker Witness, 1944
Nature and Artifice, 1979
The Need for a Study on the Psychology of Disarmament, 1964
The Need for a University of the Building Industry, 1969
The Need for Reform of National Income Statistics, 1971
Needs and Opportunities in Peace Research and Peace Education, 1964
A New Ethos for a New Era, 1970
A New Face for the Democratic Party?, 1982
New Goals for Society? 1972
A New Look at Institutionalism, 1957
New Magazine: An Opportunity for the Membership, 1979
New Nations for Old, 1942
The Next 100 Years? 1980
The Next Thirty Years in General Systems, 1984
The Next 200 Years, 1976
The Next 200 Years: Can We Move Toward a Sustainable High-Level Society?
     1979
No Second Chance for Man, 1970
Normative Science and Agricultural Policy, 1978
A Not-So-Simple Little System, 1979
A Note on Anatol Rapoport as a Philosopher, 1979
A Note on the Consumption Function, 1935
A Note on the Future of Grants Economics, 1979
A Note on the Theory of the Black Market, 1947
Notes on a Theory of Philanthropy, 1962

Notes on Goods, Services, and Cultural Economics, 1977
Notes on the Information Concept, 1955
Notes on the Politics of Peace, 1966
Notes on the Present State of Neoclassical Economics as a Subset of the
    Orthodox, 1975
Notes on the Scope of Grants Economics, 1978
Numbers and Measurement on a Human Scale, 1980
Numbers Count, 1979

Observations on Judgment and Public Policy Decisions, 1978
On Being Rich and Being Poor: Technology and Productivity, 1980
On Dennis Pirages' "The Ecological Perspective and the Social Sciences,"
    1983
On the Virtues of Muddling Through, 1981
The Only Sure Thing About the Future is Uncertainty, 1979
The Optimum Utilization of Knowledge: Some Central Concepts, 1983
Organization and Conflict, 1957
"The Organization Man"--Fact or Fancy? 1958
Organization Theory as a Bridge Between Socialist and Capitalist
    Societies, 1973
Organizing Growth, 1959
Our Attitude Toward Revolution, 1961
Our Habitat: The Universe, 1978
Outrageous Fortune, 1976

Pacem in Terris and the World Community (with others), 1963
The Pacifism of All Sensible Men, 1940
A Pacifist View of History, 1939
Panel on Food and Development (discussion; with others), 1976
Panel on Resources and Growth (discussion; with others), 1976
Panel on the Human Future (discussion; with others), 1976
The Parameters of Politics, 1966
Parity, Charity, and Clarity: Ten Theses on Agricultural Policy, 1955
Passages: Work and Aging in America, 1978
Pathologies of Defense, 1984
Pathologies of the Public Grants Economy, 1982
Paths of Glory: A New Way With War, 1938
The Peace Movement and the Dynamics of Peace, 1977
A Peace Movement in Search of a Party, 1968
Peace Research, 1977
The Peace Research Movement, 1962
The Peculiar Economics of Water, 1966
People Eyeing 21st Century as Age When Mankind Matures, 1971
Personal and Political Peacemaking, 1944
Perspective on the Economics of Peace, 1961
Perspectives on Violence, 1983
Persuading by Threat, 1979
Philosopher: Ken Boulding (interview), 1979
The Philosophy of Peace Research, 1970
Physiology and Ecology: The Two Legs of General Systems, 1980
The Place of the "Displacement Cost" Concept in Economic Theory, 1932
The Place of the Image in the Dynamics of Society, 1964
Plains of Science, Summits of Passion, 1974
The Political Consequences of the Social Sciences, 1966
Political Implications of General Systems Research, 1961
The Political Paradox, 1981
Pondering the New Decade's Improbables, 1979
Population and Poverty, 1965

The Possibilities of Peace Research in Australia, 1964
The Possibilities of Socialism in Britain, 1932
Possible Conflicts Between Economic Stability and Economic Progress, 1955
The Power of Negative Thinking, 1978
The Power of Nonconflict, 1977
The Practice of the Love of God, 1942
The Prayer of Magic and the Prayer of Love, 1945
Predictive Reliability and the Future: The Need for Uncertainty, 1975
Preface (in Kenneth Boulding and Thomas Wilson, eds., Redistribution Through
    the Financial System), 1978
Preface (in Carlos Obregon, De la Filosofia a la Economia: Historia de la
    Armonia Social; in Spanish), 1984
Preface (in Craig W. Smith and Eric W. Skjei, Getting Grants), 1980
Preface (in Norman Walbek and Sidney Weintraub, eds., Conflict, Order, and
    Peace in the Americas: Part I), 1978
Preface (with Emile Benoit; in Emile Benoit and Kenneth Boulding, eds.,
    Disarmament and the Economy), 1963
Preface to a Special Issue, 1968
The Present Position of the Theory of the Firm, 1960
Preventing Schismogenesis (comments on Richard Flacks, "Protest or Conform:
    Some Social Psychological Perspectives on Legitimacy"), 1969
The Prevention of World War III, 1962
Price Control in a Subsequent Deflation, 1948
The Price System and the Price of the Great Society, 1967
Prices and Other Institutions, 1977
Prices and Values: Infinite Worth in a Finite World, 1979
Pricing in the Energy Crisis, 1974
The Principle of Personal Responsibility, 1954
The Problem of Consensus in American Society, 1978
The Problem of the Country Meeting, 1943
Productivity (with others), 1978
Professor Knight's Capital Theory: A Note in Reply, 1936
A Profile of the American Economy, 1966
A Program for Justice Research, 1974
Property: Whose Right?, 1982
The Prospects of Economic Abundance, 1967
Protestantism's Lost Economic Gospel, 1950
Public Choice and the Grants Economy: The Intersecting Set, 1969
The Public Image of American Economic Institutions, 1961
Publicly Supported, Universally Available Education and Equality, 1976
A Pure Theory of Conflict Applied to Organizations, 1961
A Pure Theory of Death: Dilemmas of Defense Policy in a World of
    Conditional Viability, 1962
The Pursuit of Equality, 1975
The Pursuit of Happiness and the Value of the Human Being (in Japanese),
    1971
The Puzzle of the North-South Differential, 1976

The Quaker Approach in Economic Life, 1953
Quakerism and the Arts, 1983
Quakerism in the World of the Future, 1966
The Quality of Life and Economic Affluence, 1974
Quality Versus Equality: The Dilemma of the University, 1975

Rags, Riches, and Redistribution, 1982
The Real World of the Seventies and Beyond, 1970
Realism and Sentimentalism in the Student Movement, 1964

Reality Testing and Value Orientation in International Systems: The
    Role of Research, 1965
Reciprocity and Exchange: The Individual and the Household in Society
    (in French), 1978
Reflection of the Election--An Interview with Kenneth Boulding, 1968
Reflections on Law and Justice, 1978
Reflections on Planning: The Value of Uncertainty, 1974
Reflections on Poverty, 1961
Reflections on Protest, 1965
Reflections on the Uncertain Future of Social and Community Life, 1983
Reflections on Values, Science, War and Peace: What Signs of Hope?, 1983
The Relations of Economic, Political and Social Systems, 1962
Religion and the Social Sciences, 1958
Religious Foundations of Economic Progress, 1952
Religious Perspectives of College Teaching in Economics, 1950
Replacement and Repair: Healing the Body Politic, 1977
The Report of the President (ISA), 1975
Requirements for a Social Systems Analysis of the Dynamics of the
    World War Industry, 1968
Research and Development for the Emergent Nations, 1965
Research for Peace, 1969
Response (to Gibson Winter, "Hope for the Earth"; with others), 1984
Revolution and Development, 1968
The Ripening Society, 1980
The Role of Economics in the Establishment of Stable Peace, 1968
The Role of Exemplars in the Learning of Community, 1969
The Role of Government in a Free Economy, 1982
The Role of Government in a Free Society, 1982
The Role of Households in World Development, 1982
The Role of Law in the Learning of Peace, 1963
The Role of Legitimacy in the Dynamics of Society, 1969
The Role of the Church in the Making of Community and Identity, 1969
The Role of the Museum in the Propagation of Developed Images, 1966
The Role of the Price Structure in Economic Development (with Pritam
    Singh), 1962
The Role of the Social Sciences in the Control of Technology, 1972
The Role of the Undergraduate College in Social Change, 1970
The Role of the War Industry in International Conflict, 1967
Role Prejudice as an Economic Problem, 1973

The Scarcity of Saints, 1967
Scholarly Rights and Political Morality, 1976
The Schooling Industry as a Possibly Pathological Section of the American
    Economy, 1972
Science: A World Community, 1980
Science and Its Social Environment, 1981
Science and National Defense: A Speculative Essay and Discussion, 1982
Science and the Christian Phylum in Evolutionary Tension, 1983
Science and Uncertain Futures, 1979
Science: Our Common Heritage, 1980
Science, Technology, and Our Environment (in Japanese), 1982
The Sciences and the Humanities: Kindred Activities, 1979
Scientific Nomenclature, 1960
The Scientific Revelation, 1970
A Second Look at Progress and Poverty, 1982
Secular Images of Man in the Social Sciences, 1958
A Service of National Importance, 1940
The Shadow of the Stationary State, 1973

The Skills of the Economist, 1953
The Skills of the Economist (in Portuguese), 1954
Skinner: A Dissident View (comments on B.F. Skinner, "Selection by
    Consequences"), 1984
Social Dynamics, 1973
Social Dynamics in West Indian Society, 1961
Social Justice in Social Dynamics, 1962
Social Risk, Political Uncertainty, and the Legitimacy of Private Profit,
    1973
Social Sciences, 1965
The Social Sciences and Human Development, 1982
The Social System and the Energy Crisis, 1974
Social Systems Analysis and the Study of International Conflict, 1970
The Society of Abundance, 1963
Sociobiology or Biosociology? 1978
Some Contributions of Economics to the General Theory of Value, 1956
Some Contributions of Economics to Theology and Religion, 1957
Some Difficulties in the Concept of Economic Input, 1961
Some Functions of the Grants Economy, 1970
Some Hesitant Reflections on the Political Future, 1970
Some Observations on the Learning of Economics, 1975
Some Questions on the Measurement and Evaluation of Organization, 1962
Some Reflections on Inflation and Economic Development, 1957
Some Reflections on Stewardship, 1940
Some Unsolved Problems in Economic Education, 1969
Sources of Reasonable Hope for the Future, 1984
Space as a Factor of Production, 1981
Spaceship Earth Revisited, 1980
The Specialist With a Universal Mind, 1968
A Spectrum of Strategies for Research Grants, 1975
A Sporting Chance, 1976
The Spotted Reality: The Fragmentation, Isolation, and Conflict in Today's
    World, 1966
The Sputnik Within, 1968
Stability in International Systems: The Role of Disarmament and
    Development, 1969
The Stability of Inequality, 1975
Standards for Our Economic System: Discussion (with others), 1960
Statement (on Learning, Teaching, Education, and Development), 1968
Statement Before the House Committee on Science and Technology, U.S. Congress,
    1980
Statement Before the Joint Economic Committee, U.S. Congress, 1978
Statement Before the Select Subcommitee on Education of the House Committee on
    Education and Labor, U.S. Congress, 1970
Statement Before the Subcommittee of the Senate Committee on Foreign
    Relations, U.S. Congress, 1956
Statement Before the Subcommittee on Agricultural Policy of the Joint
    Economic Committee, U.S. Congress, 1958
Statement Before the Subcommittee on Economy in Government of the Joint
    Economic Committee, U.S. Congress, 1969
Statement Before the Subcommittee on Fiscal Policy of the Joint Economic
    Committee, U.S. Congress, 1965
Statement to the Continuing Committee (AAAS Global Seminar), 1984
Structure and Stability: The Economics of the Next Adjustment, 1956
Study of the Soviet Economy: Its Place in American Education (discussion;
    with others), 1961
Successes and Failures, 1978
Survival at Gunpoint, 1981

Symbol, Substance, and the Moral Economy, 1978
Symbols for Capitalism, 1959
System Analysis and Its Use in the Classroom (with Alfred Kuhn and
     Lawrence Senesh), 1973
System Theory, Mathematics, and Quantification, 1983

The Task of the Teacher in the Social Sciences, 1969
Taxation in War Time: Some Implications for Friends, 1942
Taxes Can Be Fun, 1977
Technology and the Changing Social Order, 1969
Technology and the Integrative System, 1967
A Technology for Educational Art? 1975
Technology in the Evolutionary Process, 1983
Technology in the Perspective of Societal Evolution (in German), 1981
The Theory and Measurement of Price Expectations: Discussion (with others),
     1949
The Theory of a Single Investment, 1935
The Theory of Human Betterment, 1974
A Theory of Prediction Applied to the Future of Economic Growth, 1973
A Theory of Small Society, 1960
The Theory of the Firm in the Last Ten Years, 1942
Third Plenary Session: Panel Discussion (with others), 1979
This Sporting Life, 1977
The Threat System, 1969
The Threatening Economy (with others), 1979
Three Concepts of Disarmament, 1958
The Three Faces of Power, 1972
Time and Investment, 1936
Time and Investment: Reply, 1936
Times and Seasons, 1945
To Cultivate Our Garden, 1978
Toward a General Theory of Growth, 1953
Toward a Modest Society: The End of Growth and Grandeur, 1971
Toward a Normative Science, 1977
Toward a Rethinking of the Quaker Message, 1979
Toward a Theory for the Study of Community, 1972
Toward a Theory of Discrimination, 1976
Toward a Theory of Peace, 1964
Toward a Theory of Research Grants? 1975
Toward a Vintage Society, 1980
Toward an Evolutionary Theology, 1981
Toward an Evolutionary Theology, 1984
Toward the Development of a Cultural Economics, 1972
Toward the Year 2000, 1971
Towards a Pure Theory of Foundations, 1972
Towards a Pure Theory of Threat Systems, 1963
Towards a Sustainable Society: The Transition to Human Maturity, 1976
Towards a Twenty-First Century Politics, 1972
Towards the Development of a Security Community in Europe, 1966
Town and Country Interviews Dr. Kenneth Boulding, 1968
Trim "War Industry," Help the Economy, 1975
Truth or Power? 1975
Twenty-Five Theses on Peace and Trade, 1954
The "Two Cultures," 1967
Two Principles of Conflict, 1964

Undoing Doomsday, 1982
The Unimportance of Energy, 1982

Universal, Policed Disarmament as the Only Stable System of National
    Defense, 1958
The Universe as a General System, 1977
Universities in an Evolutionary Environment, 1976
Universities, University Knowledge, and the Human Future, 1974
The University and Tomorrow's Civilization: Its Role in the Development
    of a World Community, 1967
The University as an Economic and Social Unit, 1968
The University, Society, and Arms Control, 1962
Unprofitable Empire, Britain in India 1800-1967: A Critique of the Hobson-
    Lenin Thesis on Imperialism (with Tapan Mukerjee), 1971
The U.S. and Revolution, 1961
The Uses of Price Theory, 1963

Values, Technology, and Divine Legitimation, 1968
The Veracity of Outwardness, 1977
Verifiability of Economic Images, 1966
Violence and Revolution: Some Reflections on Cuba, 1960

Wages as a Share in the National Income, 1951
The Wages of Sin, 1980
War as a Public Health Problem: Conflict Management as a Key to Survival,
    1965
War as an Economic Institution, 1962
War as an Investment: The Strange Case of Japan (with Alan H. Gleason),
    1965
The War Industry, 1979
The War Industry and the American Economy, 1970
The Weapon as an Element in the Social System, 1972
Welcome (in Federal R&D/R&D, Industry, & the Economy), 1979
Welcome to Our Annual Meeting (AAAS), 1980
Welding and Nondestructive Testing of Social Systems, 1979
Welfare Economics, 1952
What About Christian Economics? 1951
What Are Resources? 1975
What Can We Know and Teach About Social Systems? 1968
What Do Economic Indicators Indicate? Quality and Quantity in the
    GNP, 1971
What Do We Know When We Know a Number? 1975
What Don't We Know That Hurts Us? 1969
What Hope for Peace? (in Japanese), 1982
What is Economic Progress? (in French), 1961
What Is Loyalty? 1942
What Is the GNP Worth? 1970
What Lies Ahead? 1940
What Went Wrong, If Anything, Since Copernicus? 1974
Where Are We Going, If Anywhere? A Look at Post-Civilization, 1962
Where Do We Go From Here, If Anywhere? 1961
Where Do We Go From Here?--Reflections on Possible Futures, 1979
Where Does Development Lead? 1971
Where Is the Labor Movement Moving? 1945
Why Did Gandhi Fail? 1964
The Wisdom of Man and the Wisdom of God, 1966
Women Employed: Impact on the Family (with others), 1977
Wood in the Energy Economy, 1977
The World as an Economic Region, 1974
The World Community of Scholars: Reflections on the Delhi Global Seminar
    of December 1980

World Economic Contacts and National Policies, 1948
World Society: The Range of Possible Futures, 1983
The World War Industry as an Economic Problem, 1963
A World-Famous "Economist-Philosopher" Gives His Views on Religion,
    Radicalism . . . (interview), 1971
Worship and Fellowship, 1938

Yes, Virginia, There Will Be a Year 2000, 1977

BOOKS BY TITLE

The Appraisal of Change (in Japanese), 1972
Beasts, Ballads, and Bouldingisms: A Collection of Writings by Kenneth
    E. Boulding, Richard P. Beilock, ed., 1980
Beyond Economics: Essays on Society, Religion, and Ethics, 1968
Conflict and Defense: A General Theory, 1962
Disarmament and the Economy (edited with Emile Benoit), 1963
Ecodynamics: A New Theory of Societal Evolution, 1978
Economic Analysis, 1941; revised ed., 1948; 3rd ed., 1955; 4th ed., 1966
Economic Imperialism: A Book of Readings (edited with Tapan Mukerjee),
    1972
Economics as a Science, 1970
The Economics of Human Betterment (edited), 1984
The Economics of Peace, 1945; reprinted, 1972)
The Economy of Love and Fear: A Preface to Grants Economics, 1973
Evolutionary Economics, 1981
General Systems: Yearbook of the Society for General Systems Research,
    Vol. XXIII (edited with H.R. Porter), 1979
The Image: Knowledge in Life and Society, 1956
The Impact of the Social Sciences, 1966
Kenneth E. Boulding Collected Papers: Vol. I: Economics (1932-1955), Fred R.
    Glahe, ed., 1971; Vol. II: Economics (1956-1970), Fred R. Glahe, ed.,
    1971; Vol. III: Political Economy, Larry D. Singell, ed., 1973;
    Vol. IV: Toward a General Social Science, Larry D. Singell, ed., 1974;
    Vol. V: International Systems: Peace, Conflict Resolution and Politics,
    Larry D. Singell, ed., 1975; Vol. VI: Toward the Twenty-First Century:
    Political Economy, Social Systems, and World Peace, Larry D. Singell,
    ed., 1985
Linear Programming and the Theory of the Firm (edited with W. Allen
    Spivey), 1960
The Meaning of the Twentieth Century: The Great Transition, 1964
The Optimum Utilization of Knowledge: Making Knowledge Serve Human
    Betterment (edited with Lawrence Senesh), 1983
The Organizational Revolution: A Study in the Ethics of Economic
    Organization, 1953
Peace and the War Industry (edited), 1970; 2nd ed., 1973
A Preface to Grants Economics: The Economy of Love and Fear, 1981
A Primer on Social Dynamics: History as Dialectics and Development,
    1970
Principles of Economic Policy, 1958
The Prospering of Truth, 1970
Readings in Price Theory, Vol. VI (edited with George J. Stigler), 1952
A Reconstruction of Economics, 1950

Redistribution Through the Financial System: The Grants Economics of
     Money and Credit (edited with Thomas F. Wilson), 1978
Redistribution to the Rich and the Poor: The Grants Economics of
     Income Distribution (edited with Martin Pfaff), 1972
The Skills of the Economist, 1958
The Social System of the Planet Earth (with Elise Boulding and Guy M.
     Burgess), prelim. ed., 1977; 1980
Sonnets from the Interior Life and Other Autobiographical Verse, 1975
Stable Peace, 1978
There is a Spirit (The Nayler Sonnets), 1945; 5th printing, 1975
Transfers in an Urbanized Economy: Theories and Effects of the Grants
     Economy (edited with Martin and Anita Pfaff), 1973

BOOK REVIEWS BY AUTHOR

Ackerman. See: Johnson, 1959
Allais, Économie et Intérêt, 1951
Ardant. See: Mendes-France, 1955
Ardrey, The Territorial Imperative: A Personal Inquiry into the Animal
     Origins of Property and Nations, 1967
Arendt, The Human Condition, 1960
_____, On Violence, 1971
Arnhym. See: Power, 1965
Aron, Introduction to the Philosophy of History, 1961
Ayres, Toward a Reasonable Society, 1962
Axelrod, The Evolution of Cooperation, 1984

Bahr et al., eds., Population Resources and the Future Non-Malthusian
     Perspectives, 1973
Bain, Barriers to New Competition: Their Character and Consequences in
     Manufacturing Industries, 1957
Balk, The Religion Business, 1969
Balogh, The Irrelevance of Conventional Economics, 1983
Barnet, The Lean Years: Politics in the Age of Scarcity, 1981
Bauer, ed., Social Indicators, 1967
Bay, The Structure of Freedom, 1960
Baykov, The Development of the Soviet Economic System, 1946
Bazelon, The Paper Economy, 1965
Beaufre, Deterrence and Strategy, 1968
Beer, Peace Against War: The Ecology of International Violence, 1984
Behrens III. See: Meadows et al., 1972
Bell, The Coming of Post-Industrial Society, A Venture in Social Forecasting,
     1974
Belshaw, The Sorcerer's Apprentice: An Anthropology of Public Policy, 1977
Benjamin, The Limits of Politics: Collective Goods and Political Change
     in Postindustrial Societies, 1980
Benoit, Defense and Economic Growth in Developing Countries, 1974
Bhagwati, ed., Economics and World Order: From the 1970's to the 1990's, 1973
Biet, Theories Contemporaines du Profit, 1959
Black, The Dynamics of Modernization: A Study in Comparative History, 1968
Blumberg, Inequality in an Age of Decline, 1981
Bonner, Cells and Societies, 1956
Boulding, Ecodynamics: A New Theory of Societal Evolution (2 reviews), 1983
Brady, Business as a System of Power, 1944

Braybrooke and Lindblom, A Strategy of Decision: Policy Evaluation as a
     Social Process, 1964 and 1969
Breit and Culbertson, eds., Science and Ceremony: The Institutional
     Economics of C.E. Ayres, 1977
Breit and Ransom, The Academic Scribblers: American Economists in Collision,
     1973
Brill, "Social Accounting and Economic Analysis," 1952
Brodie, War & Politics, 1974
Bronfenbrenner, Income Distribution Theory, 1972
Brown, Building a Sustainable Society, 1982
_____, World Without Borders, 1973
Brunner and Markowitz, "Stocks and Flows in Monetary Analysis," 1952
Burns, ed., Wesley Clair Mitchell, The Economic Scientist, 1952

Calder, ed., Unless Peace Comes: A Scientific Forecast of New Weapons, 1969
Chadwick. See: Bahr et al., 1973
Chamberlain, A General Theory of Economic Process, 1956
Chammah. See: Rapoport, 1966
Checkland, Systems Thinking, Systems Practice, 1982
Clark, J., Competition as a Dynamic Process, 1962
_____, Economic Institutions and Human Welfare, 1957
Clark, W. Energy for Survival: The Alternative to Extinction, 1974
Coase, British Broadcasting, 1951
Cochran, The American Business System: A Historical Perspective, 1900-1955
     (with John Kenneth Galbraith),
     1958
Cohen and Cyert, Theory of the Firm: Resource Allocation in a Market
     Economy, 1966
Cole, A., Business Enterprise in Its Social Setting, 1959
Cole, H. et al., eds., Models of Doom: A Critique of the Limits to Growth,
     1973
Coleman, Introduction to Mathematical Sociology, 1966
Collard, Altruism and Economy: A Study in Non-Selfish Economics, 1979
Colm, The American Economy in 1960 (with others), 1953; correction and
     apology, 1954
Commoner, The Poverty of Power: Energy and the Economic Crisis, 1976
Cook Lectures on American Institutions, 1951
Cowles Commission, Economic Theory and Measurement: Twenty Year Research
     Report, 1932-1952, 1953
Culbertson. See: Breit, 1977
Cyert. See: Cohen, 1966
_____ and March, A Behavioral Theory of the Firm, 1964

Davis. See: Miller et al., 1964
DeChazeau et al., Jobs and Markets: How to Prevent Inflation and Depression
     in the Transition, 1947
de Grazia, Of Time, Work, and Leisure, 1963
de Koster, All Ye That Labor: An Essay on Christianity, Communism, and the
     Problem of Evil, 1957
De Schweinitz, Jr., Industrialization and Democracy: Economic Necessities
     and Political Possibilities, 1965
Dean, Test Ban and Disarmament, 1968
Demant, Religion and the Decline of Capitalism, 1953
Deutsch. See: Wright et al., 1963
Dietze, Youth, University, and Democracy, 1971
Dimock, The New American Political Economy, 1962

Drucker, The Age of Discontinuity: Guidelines to Our Changing Society, 1970
_____, The Unseen Revolution: How Pension Fund Socialism Came to America, 1977
Duff, The Social Thought of the World Council of Churches, 1956
Duncan, Communication and Social Order, 1963
Dunn, Jr., Economic and Social Development: A Process of Social Learning, 1973

Easton, A Systems Analysis of Political Life, 1968
Eckstein, ed., Comparison of Economic Systems: Theoretical and Methodological Approaches, 1974
Elkan, The New Model Economy: Economic Inventions for the Rest of the Century, 1984
Eulau, Technology and Civility: The Skill Revolution in Politics, 1978
Evan. See: Wright et al., 1963
Ewald, Jr., ed., Environment and Change: The Next Fifty Years, 1970
_____, ed., Environment and Policy: The Next Fifty Years, 1970

Fackler. See: Miller et al., 1964
Finer, Road To Reaction, 1946
Forrester, World Dynamics, 1972
Fourastié, The Causes of Wealth, 1961
Freeman. See: Cole et al., 1973
Fried et al., eds., War: The Anthropology of Armed Conflict and Aggression, 1969
Friedman, Capitalism and Freedom, 1963
_____, Essays in Positive Economics, 1954

Galbraith, The Affluent Society, 1959
_____, Economics & the Public Purpose, 1974
_____, The New Industrial State (2 reviews), 1967
Galtung, Essays in Peace Research: Vols. I and II, 1977
Georgescu-Roegen, The Entropy Law and the Economic Process, 1972
Gilpin, War and Change in World Politics, 1983
Grace, The Concept of Property in Modern Christian Thought, 1954
Green, Deadly Logic: The Theory of Nuclear Deterrence, 1967
Gustavson, The Institutional Drive, 1967

Haas and Whiting, Dynamics of International Relations, 1964
Haavelmo, A Study in the Theory of Economic Evolution: Contributions to Economic Analysis, III, 1955
Halle, The Society of Man, 1967
Hardin, Exploring New Ethics for Survival: The Voyage of the Spaceship Beagle, 1972
_____, Naked Emperors: Essays of a Taboo-Stalker, 1983
Harris. See: Fried et al., 1969
Hart. See: DeChazeau et al., 1947
Heilbroner, The Limits of American Capitalism, 1967
Henderson, A., The Innovative Spirit, 1971
Henderson, H., Creating Alternative Futures: The End of Economics, 1984
Herzog, The Church Trap, 1969
Hickman and Kuhn, Individuals, Groups, and Economic Behavior, 1956
Hicks, A Theory of Economic History, 1970
_____, Value and Capital, An Inquiry into Some Fundamental Principles of Economic Theory, 1939
Higgins, What Do Economists Know? 1953
Hitch and McKean, The Economics of Defense in the Nuclear Age, 1961

Hobsbawm, Industry and Empire: An Economic History of Britain Since 1750, 1971
Homans, Social Behavior: Its Elementary Forms, 1962
Horowitz, D., Empire and Revolution: A Radical Interpretation of Contemporary History, 1969
Horowitz, I., and Katz, Social Science and Public Policy in the United States, 1977
Hudson, Super Imperialism: The Economic Strategy of American Empire, 1972

Iklé, Every War Must End, 1972
_____, How Nations Negotiate, 1966
Ilchman. See: Uphoff, 1970
Instituto Brasileiro dé Economia da Fundacão Getúlio Vargas, Contribuicões à Análise do Disenvolvimento Econômico (Festschrift in honor of Eugenio Gudin), 1958

Jahoda. See: Cole et al., 1973
James, The Death of Progress, 1973
Janeway, The Economics of Crisis: War, Politics, and the Dollar, 1968
Jewkes, Public and Private Enterprise, 1967
Johnson, F., and Ackerman, The Church as Employer, Money Raiser and Investor, 1959
Johnson, H., On Economics and Society, 1976

Kahn, Thinking About the Unthinkable, 1962
_____, World Economic Development: 1979 and Beyond, 1981
_____ and Wiener, The Year 2000: A Framework for Speculation on the Next Thirty-Three Years, 1968
Kaplan, System and Process in International Politics, 1958
Katz. See: Horowitz, 1977
Kiernan, Marxism and Imperialism, 1977
Knorr and Verba, eds., The International System: Theoretical Essays, 1963
Krenz, Energy: From Opulence to Sufficiency, 1981
Kuhn, A., The Study of Society: A Unified Approach, 1964
Kuhn, M. See: Hickman, 1956
Kurth. See: Rosen, 1977

LaPaix, Recueils de la Société Jean Bodin, 1964
Lachmann, Capital and Its Structure, 1956
Lange, Wholes and Parts: A General Theory of System Behavior, 1966
Lapp, The Logarithmic Century, 1973
Lauterbach, Man, Motives, and Money: Psychological Frontiers of Economics, 1955
Lave, Technological Change: Its Conception and Measurement, 1967
Lebergott, The American Economy: Income, Wealth, and Want, 1976
Leites and Wolf, Jr., Rebellion and Authority: An Analytic Essay on Insurgent Conflicts, 1970
Levy et al., Urban Outcomes: Schools, Streets, and Libraries, 1975
Lincoln. See: Padelford, 1964
Lindbeck, Swedish Economic Policy, 1977
Lindblom. See: Braybrooke, 1964 and 1969
_____, Politics and Markets: The World's Political-Economic Systems, 1979
Linder, The Harried Leisure Class, 1970
Little, A Critique of Welfare Economics, 1951
Lo Bello, The Vatican Empire, 1969
Lorenz, On Aggression, 1967

Lowe, On Economic Knowledge: Toward a Science of Political Economics, 1965
Lundberg, E., Business Cycles and Economic Policy, 1958
Lundberg, F., The Rich and the Super Rich, 1968
Lutz, F. and V., The Theory of Investment of the Firm, 1953

Machlup. See: Miller et al., 1964
_____, The Production and Distribution of Knowledge in the United
        States, 1963
Mack, "Contrasts in Patterns of Flows of Commodities and Funds," 1952
MacRae, Jr., The Social Function of Social Science, 1978
Maddison, Economic Growth in the West: Comparative Experience in Europe and
        North America, 1964
Maddox, The Doomsday Syndrome, 1973
Mamdani, The Myth of Population Control: Family, Caste, and Class in an
        Indian Village, 1973
March. See: Cyert, 1964
Marcuse, An Essay on Liberation, 1969
Markowitz. See: Brunner, 1952
Mason, ed., The Corporation in Modern Society, 1960
Mayhew, Arrogance on Campus, 1971
Mazlish, ed., The Railroad and the Space Program: An Exploration in
        Historical Analogy, 1966
McCarthy, The Ultimate Folly: War by Pestilence, Asphyxiation and
        Defoliation, 1969
McClelland, College Teaching of International Relations, 1964
McKean. See: Hitch, 1961
McLuhan, The Gutenberg Galaxy: The Making of Typographic Man, 1965
_____, Understanding Media, The Extensions of Man, 1965
Mead, Culture and Commitment: A Study of the Generation Gap, 1970
Meade, The Growing Economy, 1969
Meadows, D. and D. et al., The Limits to Growth, 1972
Means. See: DeChazeau et al., 1947
_____, Pricing Power and the Public Interest: A Study Based on Steel, 1962
Medawar, The Future of Man: Predictions of a Biologist, 1961
Meier, Science and Economic Development: New Patterns of Living, 1957
Meisel, The Myth of the Ruling Class: Gaetano Mosca and the "Elite," 1958
Melko, 52 Peaceful Societies, 1976
Meltsner. See: Levy et al., 1975
Mendes-France and Ardant, Economics and Action, 1955
Mendlovitz, ed., On the Creation of a Just World Order: Preferred Worlds for
        the 1990's, 1976
Merton, On the Shoulders of Giants; A Shandean Postscript, 1966
Mesarovic and Pestel, Mankind at the Turning Point, 1975
Mesthene, Technological Change: Its Impact on Man and Society, 1970
Miller, M., et al., eds., Fritz Machlup, Essays on Economic Semantics, 1964
Miller, J., Living Systems, 1979
Millis, An End To Arms, 1965
Mitchell. See: Burns, ed., 1952
Morgan, Observations, 1969
Morgenthau, Politics Among Nations, 1964
Murphy. See: Fried et al., 1969
Myers. See: DeChazeau et al., 1947
Myrdal, Asian Drama: An Inquiry into the Poverty Nations, 1968
_____, Beyond the Welfare State: Economic Planning and Its International
        Implications, 1961
_____, An International Economy: Problems and Prospects, 1956

National Bureau of Economic Research, Studies in Income and Wealth,
    Vol. 13, 1952
Nelson and Winter, An Evolutionary Theory of Economic Change, 1984
Niebuhr, The Structure of Nations and Empires, 1960
Nieburg, In the Name of Science, 1967
Novick, The Careless Atom, 1969
Nygaard, America Prays, 1946

Odum, H. and E., Energy Basis for Man and Nature, 1977
Okun, The Political Economy of Prosperity, 1970
Olson, Jr., The Logic of Collective Action, 1969
Organski, World Politics, 1964

Padelford and Lincoln, The Dynamics of International Politics, 1964
Parsons, Structure and Process in Modern Societies, 1961
_____ and Platt, The American University, 1975
_____ and Smelser, Economy and Society: A Study in the Integration of
    Economic and Social Theory, 1957
Paton, Shirtsleeve Economics, 1962
Pavitt. See Cole et al., 1973
Perlo, Militarism and Industry -- Arms Profiteering in the Missile Age, 1963
Pestel. See: Mesarovic, 1975
Peterson, The Industrial Order and Social Policy, 1973
Platt, G. See: Parsons, 1975
Platt, J., Perception and Change: Projections for Survival, 1971
Polak, The Image of the Future, Vols. I and II, 1962
Power, with Arnhym, Design for Survival, 1965
Price, The Scientific Estate, 1966
Pryor, The Origins of the Economy: A Comparative Study of Distribution
    in Primitive and Peasant Economies, 1979

Quandt. See: Thorp, 1960

Rae, American Automobile Manufacturers: The First Forty Years, 1959
Randall, Economics and Public Policy, 1955
_____, A Foreign Economic Policy for the United States, 1955
Randers. See: Meadows et al., 1972
Ransom. See: Breit, 1973
Rapoport, Conflict in Man-Made Environment, 1975
_____, Strategy and Conscience, 1964
_____ and Chammah, Prisoner's Dilemma: A Study in Conflict and
    Cooperation, 1966
Rawls, A Theory of Justice, 1973
Report from Iron Mountain on the Possibility and Desirability of Peace, 1968
Rescher, Scientific Progress: A Philosophical Essay on the Economics
    of Research in Natural Science, 1980
Riddell, Ecodevelopment: Economics, Ecology and Development, 1982
Rifkin, Entropy: A New World View, 1980
Roberts and Stephenson, Marx's Theory of Exchange, Alienation and
    Crisis, 1975
Robertson, Should Churches Be Taxed? 1969
Robinson, Economic Heresies: Some Old-Fashioned Questions in Economic
    Theory, 1971
_____, Economic Philosophy, 1963
Roose, The Economics of Recession and Revival, 1954
Röpke, The Social Crisis of Our Time, 1950
Rosen and Kurth, eds., Testing Theories of Economic Imperialism, 1977

Rosenau, ed., International Politics and Foreign Policy: A Reader in Research and Theory, 1964
Rostow, Politics and the Stages of Growth, 1971
Russett, What Price Vigilance? The Burdens of National Defense, 1972
_____, ed., Economic Theories of International Politics, 1969

Sampson, The Discovery of Peace, 1974
Samuelson, Foundations of Economic Analysis, 1948
Samuelsson, Religion and Economic Action, 1962
Schelling, The Strategy of Conflict, 1961
Schleicher, International Relations, 1964
Schmid, Property, Power, and Public Choice: An Inquiry Into Law and Economics, 1979
Schneider, Destiny of Change: How Relevant is Man in the Age of Development? 1969
Schramm, Responsibility in Mass Communication, 1958
Schultz, The Theory of Measurement of Demand, 1939
Scitovsky, The Joyless Economy: An Inquiry Into Human Satisfaction, 1977
Seckler, Thorstein Veblen and the Institutionalists: A Study in the Social Philosophy of Economics, 1976
Selden, ed., Capitalism and Freedom: Problems and Prospects, 1976
Seligman, Most Notorious Victory: Man in an Age of Automation, 1967
_____, Permanent Poverty: An American Syndrome, 1968
Shackle, Epistemics & Economics: A Critique of Economic Doctrines, 1973
_____, A Scheme of Economic Theory, 1967
Sharp, The Politics of Non-Violent Action, 1974
Sievers, Revolution, Evolution and the Economic Order, 1962
Simon, The Ultimate Resource, 1982
Slichter, The American Economy: Its Problems and Prospects, 1949
Smelser. See: Parsons, 1957
Solo, Economic Organizations and Social Systems, 1967
Sowell, Say's Law: An Historical Analysis, 1975
Sporn, Technology, Engineering, and Economics, 1969
Stein. See: DeChazeau et al, 1947
_____, The Fiscal Revolution in America, 1970
Stephenson. See: Roberts, 1975
Stigler, The Citizen and the State: Essays on Regulation, 1976
Stoessinger, The Might of Nations, 1964

Tarshis, The Elements of Economics, 1948
Taylor, The Classical Liberalism, Marxism, and the Twentieth Century, 1960
Thayer, An End To Hierarchy! 1975
Thomas. See: Bahr et al., 1973
Thorp and Quandt, The New Inflation, 1960
Thurow, Generating Inequality: Mechanisms of Distribution in the U.S. Economy, 1976
Tufte, Political Control of the Economy, 1979
Tullock, The Organization of Inquiry, 1968

Uphoff and Ilchman, eds., The Political Economy of Change: Theoretical and Empirical Contributions, 1970

Valk, Production, Pricing, and Unemployment in the Static State, 1938
van Dorp, A Simple Theory of Capital, Wages, and Profit or Loss, 1937
Verba. See: Knorr, 1963
Vickers, The Undirected Society: Essays on the Human Implications of Industrialisation in Canada, 1960

Walter, Terror and Resistance: A Study of Political Violence, 1971
Ward, Progress for a Small Planet, 1979
____, Space Ship Earth, 1966
Warner, The Corporation in the Emergent American Society, 1963
West, Education and the State: A Study in Political Economy, 1966
Whitaker, The Philanthropoids: Foundations and Society, 1974
Whiting. See: Haas, 1964
Wiener, A. See: Kahn, 1968
Wiener, N., The Human Use of Human Beings: Cybernetics and Society, 1952
Wildavsky. See: Levy et al., 1975
Wilson, An Opening Way, 1961
Winter. See: Nelson, 1984
Wolf, Jr. See: Leites, 1970
Woodward, The Human Dilemma, 1973
Wright, D., The Economics of Disturbance, 1948
Wright, Q. et al., eds., Preventing World War III, 1963

Yntema. See: DeChazeau et al., 1947

Zipf, Human Behavior and the Principle of Least Effort, 1951

VERSE BY TITLE

Arden House Poetry, 1963
A Ballad of Ecological Awareness, 1972
A Ballade of Augsburg, 1978
The Brandywine River Anthology, 1958
The Busted Thermostat, 1952
The Conservationist's Lament; The Technologist's Reply, 1955
COPRED, A Prophecy, 1973
The Ditchley Bank Anthology, 1969
The Feather River Anthology, 1966
Isaac Watts Revised, 1976
Minutes and Comments (Symposium on Colorado Futures), 1982
The Nayler Sonnets, 1944
New Goals for Society? 1972
The Old Agricultural Lag, 1967
Reflections (on the National Conference on Managing the Environment),
    1973
Reply (to Fred L. Pryor, "When Boulding Sleeps . . ."), 1978
A Shelter for All, 1961
A Small Hymn to Science, 1981
Some Reflections (on the 4th National Study Conference on the Church
    and Economic Life), 1962
Sonnet (on the creation of an Institute of Peace), 1984
Sonnet For Prayer, 1983
Sonnets From Laxenburg: On the Numbers From Zero to Ten, 1981
Summaries (of the Second Systems Symposium), 1964
Summary (of the Conference on Economic Development, Poverty, and
    Income Distribution), 1977
Summary (of the Range of Human Conflict: A Symposium), 1966
T.R., 1958

There Is a Spirit. See: The Nayler Sonnets, 1944
Thoughts at the AAAS Workshop on the Role of Scientific and Engineering
     Societies in Development, 1979
Verse from the WATTec 6th Annual Energy Conference and Exhibition, 1979
X Cantos, 1969